Labrys & Horns

An Introduction to

Modern Minoan Paganism

Laura Perry

Potnia Press

Dedication

To all the gods.

πάνσι θεοίς

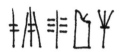

Also by Laura Perry:

Non-fiction:

The Minoan Coloring Book
The Minoan Tarot (published by Schiffer Publishing)
Ariadne's Thread: Awakening the Wonders of the Ancient
     Minoans in Our Modern Lives
The Wiccan Wellness Book: Natural Healthcare for Mind, Body,
     and Spirit, now in its second edition
Ancient Spellcraft: From the Hymns of the Hittites to the Carvings
     of the Celts, now in its second edition

Fiction:

The Last Priestess of Malia
The Bed
Jaguar Sky

LauraPerryAuthor.com

Table of Contents

List of Illustrations

Acknowledgments

My special thanks go to the members of Ariadne's Tribe, the Facebook group that's the official public forum of Modern Minoan Paganism. I wrote this book at their request. Their encouragement and enthusiasm keep me moving forward along this path.

As with any spiritual practice that relies on information from the past, Modern Minoan Paganism leans heavily on the work of archaeologists from the late 19th century to the present day. I'm indebted to all of them for their passion about the people and culture of ancient Crete and for their willingness to share their finds with the world.

I'm also grateful to my fellow writers, Pagan and otherwise. Both individually and in writers' groups, they've shared the kind of wisdom and support that can only come from those who walk the path of words.

Of course, I must thank my husband and daughter. They've been generous in their patience with both my spiritual practice (*Where* do you want to build a labyrinth?) and my writing (You want to do *what* for your research?). They've both been unfailingly supportive, and I'm blessed to have them in my life.

Most of all, I must thank the gods and my ancestors, the ultimate source of my inspiration and strength. I'm doing my best to follow honorably in their footsteps and bring the spirituality of the ancient Minoans to life again in the modern world.

Preface to the Second Edition

When I started the Facebook group Ariadne's Tribe back in 2014, I had no idea that my desire to connect with fellow Minoan enthusiasts would result in the birth of a new tradition. Along with that development came the need for a single resource that followers of Modern Minoan Paganism could refer to for their spiritual practice. That's how I came to write the first edition of *Labrys & Horns*.

It has been four eventful years since that first edition was released. In that time, Modern Minoan Paganism has solidified as a tradition. We now have a Board of Directors, a set of Official Policies, a website (ariadnestribe.wordpress.com), and our first chapters and members. On top of that, we've discovered new deities, added new festivals to our sacred calendar, and developed a standard ritual format that anyone can use, alone or with a group.

That's enough change to warrant some major revisions and updates to this book. I've left the overall format the same; the chapters are still in the same order as in the first edition. So if you read the first edition, you should be able to find your way around this one pretty easily. And if you're new to *Labrys & Horns*, I hope you find the organization easy to understand.

I use the abbreviations BCE and CE instead of BC and AD. BC (Before Christ) and AD (Anno Domini, Latin for "the year of the Lord") refer to dates that are important to Christianity, while BCE and CE simply refer to "Before the Common Era" and "Common Era." Yes, I realize the two sets of abbreviations cover the same time periods and switch over in the same year. But I think it behooves us to make choices that reflect the fact that there's more than just one religion in the world.

The awesome folks at NASA tell us that we should capitalize the names of our Earth, Sun, and Moon the same way we capitalize the names of other planets (Jupiter, Neptune), stars (Aldebaran, Sirius), and planetary moons (Io, Europa). I think it's only right that we show as much respect for our Earth, Sun, and Moon as we do the other celestial bodies, so I'll be capitalizing them in this book.

Please note that there are some differences between the information in this new second edition of *Labrys & Horns* and the first edition, and also between this book and *Ariadne's Thread*, which I have been unable to update due to the publisher's decisions. The symbolism, iconography, and deity and ritual information in *this* book are current and accurate for Modern Minoan Paganism at the time of publication and will remain so for the foreseeable future. In other words, if you're trying to pick a single reference for the practice of Modern Minoan Paganism, this new second edition of *Labrys & Horns* is your best choice.

The first few years of our journey as a spiritual tradition have been filled with the blessings of the divine and the beauty of shared community. May the future of Modern Minoan Paganism continue in that vein.

Introduction

The labrys and sacred horns are familiar symbols to many Pagans. They come from the world of the ancient Minoans who lived in the cities, villages, and countryside of Crete more than 3000 years ago. This unique culture and spirituality still speak to us today. In fact, they're especially relevant as we grapple with modern issues like gender equality and respect for the environment.

The Minoans were different from a lot of their ancient neighbors: their society and religion celebrated women and men equally. The strong, independent goddesses of the Minoan pantheon stand level with the gods. Ancient Crete wasn't a utopia by any means, but the Minoans' beliefs and practices still offer us many opportunities to celebrate the balance between the divine feminine and the divine masculine, as well as to recognize that a gender binary isn't necessarily the only way to view the world — just ask Dionysus, who shows up as a teenage boy, a grown man, a teenage girl, and a goat! Modern Minoan Paganism (MMP) also presents us with unique ways to connect with nature and find the sacred within it, from the soil beneath our feet to the sky above our heads.

Since the Linear A script the Minoans wrote is still undeciphered, we don't have any texts we can read that date all the way back to ancient Crete. Most of what we know about Minoan spirituality and mythos was recorded by later cultures and isn't always reliable. For instance, we have bits and pieces of myth and history that have come down to us by way of the Greeks. A lot of what they wrote was purposely distorted to glorify themselves and to make the Minoans look bad. A lot of it is also confusing and contradictory because the Greeks were doing

1

their best to make sense of fragments of thousand-year-old legends and tales while still fulfilling their own political and religious goals.

We also hear about the Minoans by way of the ancient Egyptians, who admired Minoan herbal medicine enough to include remedies from Crete in Egyptian medical papyruses. And we have the roughly-translated script called Linear B, a writing system the Mycenaean Greeks adapted from Linear A toward the end of Minoan times. Even though life changed over the centuries of Minoan civilization, Linear B still gives us a good idea of the way the temple complexes, towns, and farmlands were organized. And the Linear B tablets also offer us a few god and goddess names we can work with.

Of course, we have the physical remains of Minoan society as well: the temples, the cities and towns, the cave shrines and peak sanctuaries, and all the artifacts that have been found in those places. The cups and bowls, figurines and frescoes, daggers and seal rings all give us a feel for who the Minoans were, what they valued, and how they related to the world around them and the divine as well.

We can take what we know and put it together in a way that makes sense for us in the modern world. We can fit the pieces together like a puzzle that shows us the outline of the picture, and then we can fill in the details with some of what we know about the ancient world in general. But most of all, we can use this information along with our personal experience to develop a practice of Minoan spirituality in the modern world, in a way that makes sense now.

This book doesn't include footnotes regarding where each tidbit of information came from. I'd have to footnote practically every paragraph multiple times for that, and that would be beyond cumbersome to read. The information about ancient Minoan culture and religion is based on the broad consensus of modern archaeologists, though of course what's agreed on might change in the future, just as it has done in the past. The information about the deities and practices of Modern Minoan

Paganism has come from a consensus effort of our members, working to create a revivalist spiritual tradition.

I've done my best to note the places where we've made decisions based largely on shared gnosis and group spiritual experience, and places where I'm stating my own opinion. I've also specified when we've taken useful information from classical writers, noting which writer said what. But generally speaking, none of our practices come from single sources. They're almost all based on compilations of bits and pieces of information from artifacts and historic sites as well as books and academic papers on the subjects of comparative mythology, archaeoastronomy, and dance ethnography—which we then tested by actually using them in our spiritual practice and sharing our results with each other.

The ways of MMP as detailed in this book are the combined effort of dozens of people over the course of five-plus years, all of us searching for useful information and listening as well as we can to what the gods have to say. Bear in mind that we're not trying to recreate ancient Minoan religion, but to design a modern Pagan spiritual practice in connection with the Minoan gods and goddesses.

You don't need to be a member of MMP or one of its chapters to use this book. All you need to do is read along and allow the world of the ancient Minoans to come alive for you, then follow the spirit where it leads you. I believe the gods understand that life changes over time. They know we don't live in the same kind of world we did four millennia ago. And they appreciate that we're still willing to honor them and be in relationship with them. If you'd like more information about MMP as an organization as well as a spiritual tradition, you can find our Official Policies, a list of our current board members, and more on our website: ariadnestribe.wordpress.com.

This is the gift the Minoans have bequeathed to us: their goddesses and gods, their festivals, their sacred symbols that are still vibrant and relevant today. We don't have to wear the clothes the Minoans wore or live in houses like theirs, though it might be fun to try. All we really have to do is listen to what they have to tell us and allow ourselves to connect with their vision of the divine. One thing's for sure: the Minoans themselves may have died long ago, but their gods and goddesses are still very much alive, waiting for us to reach out to them.

So let's get started.

Chapter 1:
The World of the Ancient Minoans

Like every civilization around the world and across time, the Minoans of ancient Crete had their own way of doing things, though many of the things they did will be familiar to anyone reading this book. They grew food, cooked it, and ate it. They built houses, villages, towns, temples, and tombs. They traveled and traded. They created frescoes, jewelry, pottery, and bronze figurines. But what interests us most within the pages of this book is their religion: what they believed and how they worshiped.

In order to understand Minoan spiritual beliefs and practices, we need to know a little about their culture, their climate, and the era when they lived. Once we understand the world of ancient Crete, we can begin to explore its spirituality. Let's start by figuring out where the Minoans fit among the other ancient people from their part of the world.

What Happened When

All those ancient civilizations did their thing so long ago, it can be hard for us to get our heads around exactly when any of it actually happened. Sometimes it seems like all of the ancient world occurred all at once, in a big lump a long, long time ago. Of course, that's not really the case. It can be fun to look at which cultures and societies flourished at the same time—who their neighbors were, so to speak. Let's see if we can figure out where the Minoans fit in this big puzzle.

First of all, Crete is an island in the eastern Mediterranean Sea. It's the largest island out of the hundreds that are sprinkled in the beautiful blue-green water around Greece. For about a century now, Crete has been a part of the modern nation of Greece, but that wasn't always the case, and many people from Crete even today will tell you that they're not Greek, but Cretan.

Crete was originally settled by people who came from western Anatolia (modern Turkey) way back in the Neolithic era, when agriculture was first invented. These Anatolian people weren't Indo-Europeans like the later Greeks were. Instead, they were part of what Marija Gimbutas called Old Europe, the people who were there before the Indo-Europeans came. Some of these Old Europeans migrated west and south into central Europe, the Balkans, and the Mediterranean during the Neolithic. One of those waves of migration included people who made it all the way to Crete. They built their own unique culture and religion on Crete that lasted for centuries before the early Greeks came down to the island to meet the Minoans and trade with them.

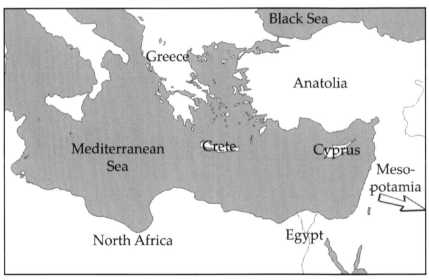

Fig. 1: Map of the Mediterranean during the Bronze Age

Although the island of Crete has been inhabited since prehistoric times, what we think of as Minoan civilization didn't begin until around 3500 BCE. At that point the people had farms, towns, and tombs but no big buildings. The heyday of the

Minoans with the sprawling temple complexes, the fancy tech (enclosed sewers, paved roads, multi-story buildings), and the beautiful artwork ran for just a few centuries, from about 1900 to 1400 BCE. The volcanic island of Thera erupted around 1600 BCE. The resulting earthquakes and tsunami did a number on the whole eastern end of the Mediterranean, including all the coastal areas of Crete. But the Minoans managed to rebuild and keep on for another couple of centuries.

In those last couple of hundred years, the Mycenaean Greeks took over the political arena, and the culture began to change. Knossos became a central power while the other cities declined. Then all the major cities on Crete, except Knossos, were systematically looted and burned somewhere between 1450 and 1400 BCE. Knossos met the same fate 50 to 100 years later. It was definitely an *interesting* time to be alive.

There were still people living on Crete after the destruction of the cities, of course, but their way of life changed so profoundly that we can't effectively call them Minoan after about 1350 BCE. We can still see the imprint of Minoan culture on the artwork for another century or two after that, then it changes enough to be unrecognizable as Minoan anymore. Around the year 1200 BCE begins an era that's called the Bronze Age collapse or, sometimes, the Greek Dark Ages. It was a time of chaos when a combination of drought, famine, and government collapse sent people migrating around the Mediterranean in search of a better life, or heading up into the hills to ride out the hard times. After that, the beautiful cities of Minoan Crete lay buried for nearly 3500 years before they were rediscovered.

So who else was on the scene while the Minoans were building their big cities and creating their beautiful artwork? The Egyptians, for one. Egypt was a vital trading partner for Crete in the ancient world. The Egyptians bought Minoan wool, olive oil, and bronze blades and they sold linen fabric, papyrus, and other goods to the people of Crete.

The Old Kingdom of Egypt began in 3100 BCE, right around the time of the rise of early Minoan civilization. That's the beginning of the pharaohs and what we think of as ancient Egypt. The heyday of the Minoans coincided with the Twelfth through the Eighteenth Dynasties in Egypt (the end of the Old Kingdom, the Second Intermediate Period, and the beginning of the New Kingdom, if you want to get technical). This was about the same time as many of the Egyptian Big Names you've probably heard of: Hatshepsut, Akhenaten, Nefertiti, Tutankhamun.

But Egypt wasn't the only place the Minoans had contact with. They traded with the people of Mesopotamia, the region around the Tigris and Euphrates river systems. That area today includes much of Iraq as well as portions of Syria and Kuwait. While the Minoans were building their way up from small villages and farms to the big cities and temple complexes, several different empires rose and fell in Mesopotamia.

The culture of Sumer in Lower Mesopotamia appeared at about the same time as early Minoan civilization. You may have heard of some of the Sumerian city-states: Ur, Lagash, Nippur, Kish. A few centuries later, while the Minoans were still perking along, Sargon of Akkad conquered the Sumerian city-states and united them, founding the Akkadian Empire. Then the Babylonian Empire arose in the same region while the Minoans were building and rebuilding their towns and temple complexes. The Babylonian King Hammurabi, with his famous laws, lived about the time the Minoans were building the first versions of the temples in Knossos, Phaistos, Malia, and Zakros.

The famous Epic of Gilgamesh, a Mesopotamian poem that counts as the oldest work of literature we've found so far, was composed while Minoan culture was at its height. If we can trust the timeline the epic gives us, the legendary King Gilgamesh lived during the same time as early Minoan civilization.

So what did the Minoans do while all these different cultures were going around them? They grew wealthy by trading. Their island didn't have a whole lot of raw materials, but they raised sheep for wool and they had a lot of talented artists and crafters. So they built ships and sailed all over, buying up raw materials like copper, tin, and semiprecious stones and selling finished goods like dyed wool cloth, bronze blades and figurines, and pottery. Back then, all trading was done by barter since coins weren't invented until almost a millennium after the destruction of the Minoan cities.

The Minoans sailed all around the Mediterranean in their ships, trading with a wide variety of people. They also appear to have braved the journey through the Straits of Gibraltar and up the Atlantic coast of Europe as far north as Britain, to get tin from Cornwall—a vital ingredient for the bronze they used to make their best-selling blades. We don't know how much the Minoans interacted with the native Britons, but we do know what was going on in the British Isles while the Minoans were busy trading. The first stage of Stonehenge was built during the early days of Minoan civilization, while the people of Crete were gathering up in towns but before they began planning their big temple complexes. The final stage of rearranging stones and dirt at Stonehenge took place during the height of Minoan culture. While the Britons were having processions around their magnificent stone circle, the Minoans were having processions down paved viaducts to their temple complexes.

But what about the Greeks? What did they have to do with the Minoans? This bit can be kind of confusing, since the island of Crete has been a part of the modern nation of Greece for about a century now, and the Greeks tend to claim Crete and the Minoans as part of Greek history. But Crete wasn't always a part of Greece. For most of its history, it was an independent island doing its own thing. DNA testing has shown that the Minoans came from the same ancestral stock as other early Europeans. These are the people who inhabited what Marija Gimbutas called Old Europe, before the Indo-Europeans came on the scene. So the Minoans weren't the same as the Indo-European Greeks—they were a separate, unique people.

As for the Greeks, there were two major Greek cultures in the ancient world. First came the Mycenaeans (the Bronze Age Greeks) who arose as a society toward the end of Minoan civilization. The Mycenaeans are the Greeks we read about in

Homer's famous works, *The Iliad* and *The Odyssey*. They flourished from about 1600 to 1100 BCE, so their society overlapped with the Minoans by two or three centuries.

And guess what? The Mycenaeans' rise is largely attributed to the influence of the Minoans. From Crete the Mycenaeans learned how to build beehive-shaped tombs, how to write, and how to improve their pottery and jewelry-making, among other things. But unlike the Minoans, their culture was warlike and profited mostly from conquest, not trade. The Mycenaeans probably also borrowed many of the Minoan gods and goddesses into their own pantheon. Rhea, Dionysus, Eileithyia, and several others began their legendary lives on Crete but eventually made their way into the Greek pantheon.

What many people don't realize is that the Mycenaeans aren't the same as the classical Greeks, the ones who gave us the famous plays and marble sculptures. Along with the rest of the eastern Mediterranean and the Near East, Mycenaean civilization collapsed around the year 1100 BCE. We don't know for sure why this happened, but it was probably due to a combination of climate problems, warfare, and the overuse of natural resources. This crumbling of cultures led to a time called the Greek Dark Ages or the Bronze Age collapse.

People still survived, of course, but there wasn't anything you could call 'high civilization'—no great art or literature and not much in the way of organized government. It wasn't until the eighth century BCE, four hundred years later, that things began to look better. This is about when Homer's famous works, *The Iliad* and *The Odyssey*, were first collected and standardized from oral traditions. And classical Greek civilization—what we usually think of when people say 'ancient Greece'—didn't reach its stride until about the fifth century BCE, a full millennium after the Minoan cities fell.

So classical Greece is very late compared to the Minoans. Their cultures didn't overlap at all, but were separated by many centuries. We hear about the Greeks because so much of their literature, architecture, and sculpture has survived. Classical revivals during the Renaissance and again during Victorian times have helped to popularize the incorrect notion that western civilization began in classical Greece. In fact, most history texts begin with the classical Greeks and don't even mention the Minoans—though they do often include the Mesopotamian cultures that flourished about the same time as Minoan civilization.

One thing to keep in mind is that we get an awful lot of our information about Minoan mythology from the Greeks, who were looking back over a chasm of a full millennium toward Minoan civilization. They took the few scraps they had—bits of writings, a few stories that had been passed down orally, some artwork that somehow wasn't destroyed when the Minoan temple complexes were looted and burned—and put them together as best they could. The world of the ancient Minoans was as lost to them as it was to us until Sir Arthur Evans began digging up the ruins of Knossos a century ago.

But of course, when the Greeks were putting those pieces together, they made sure to tweak the stories so their own society looked really good, like civilized heroes against the backdrop of the primitive Minoans. Every culture does this to some extent, so we need to bear this in mind when we're picking our way through the debris of information about Minoan religion. We need to dig up more than just temple complexes if we're going to put together a viable practice of Modern Minoan Paganism.

So really, we're looking at a few hundred years of Minoan-y goodness during the Bronze Age, which doesn't seem like a whole lot in the grand scale of history. But those few hundred years were enough to create a complex society and a fascinating, multi-layered religion that still resonates with us today. It's been just over a century since Minos Kalokairinos located Knossos and Sir Arthur Evans and his team unearthed the ruins there, but in that time Minoan culture and spirituality have captured our hearts and minds.

A Note about Seasons

Many of the people who will read this book live in the northern temperate zone: North America and the part of Europe that's north of the Mediterranean coast. We're used to four seasons: spring, summer, autumn, winter. For the places where many of us live, these are the normal yearly cycles. But it's different in the Mediterranean.

The Mediterranean Sea is ringed by lands whose climate is unique: the southern coasts of Spain and France, most of Italy and Greece, the west coast of Turkey, the Levant, and the north coast of Africa. Though these places are sectioned off on the modern map as a bunch of different nations, they belong to a single environment: the Mediterranean. This environment has its own unique set of seasons and climate. There are also a few areas of Mediterranean-type climate outside the actual Mediterranean region, for instance, in southern California, South Africa, and some parts of Australia.

Instead of four seasons, the Mediterranean climate has two: rainy and dry. The rainy season begins in the autumn and continues through a mild winter into the spring. The dry season begins in late spring and continues through summer to early autumn. Those of us who live in the northern temperate zone are used to thinking of winter as the 'dead' season, but in the Mediterranean region, the summer has that distinction. Why is that?

Because the rain stops. Really stops. And it gets baking hot. On Crete, most of the little creeks dry up and the rivers become sluggish and low. All the vegetation turns brown and crispy. Unless you have nothing to do but lie around on the beach with a lot of cool drinks at hand, it's not terribly pleasant weather. The ancient Minoans made it through those hot, dry summers without air conditioning, probably by napping through the heat of the day and sleeping on the flat roofs of their houses at night to catch any little breeze that happened by, the way many people still do around the Mediterranean today. And they were really, really glad when the cooling rains came again in the autumn.

In the four-season system, we plant our crops in the spring and harvest them in the autumn. But in the Mediterranean, field crops like grains and vegetables go in the ground in the autumn, when the rains begin. They grow throughout the autumn and the mild winter and are harvested in the spring. So the ancient Minoans actually held their harvest festivals in March or April, not September or October.

The only exception to this was the orchard crops like olives and grapes. These plants are keyed to the length of sunlight in a day, so they flower in the spring and their fruit is harvested in the autumn, even in the Mediterranean. In the days before irrigation, a particularly hot and dry summer made for a poor harvest, though apparently the Minoans did manage to dig some canals from the rivers to the farmland on their island to help protect their orchards from the blistering summer heat.

If you're practicing Modern Minoan Paganism in a northern temperate region where the agricultural season runs from March to September, you don't need to force the Mediterranean seasonal cycle onto your spirituality. You can reverse the spring and autumn festivals to match the agricultural cycle where you live. Paganism in all its forms is Earth-oriented, so acknowledging and honoring the seasons wherever you happen to live makes sense. Besides, the Minoans sailed their ships all over, so I'm sure they were familiar with climates besides the one they knew on Crete. Just remember, in the back of your mind, that the Minoans followed the seasonal cycles of the Mediterranean, and that helped to shape their spirituality as well as their culture. And don't switch any of the festival dates except the ones for planting (the New Year) and harvest.

If you live in the southern hemisphere, you'll want to celebrate the Summer and Winter Solstices when they occur in your local environment. If you live in one of the regions that has a Mediterranean climate, like southern California, you'll be able to use the MMP calendar as is, without alteration. If you live in a southern hemisphere region where the growing season runs through the summer rather than the winter, you'll want to reverse the spring and autumn festivals the way I described above. Remember, this is a nature religion: let the seasons where you live determine how you approach the sacred calendar.

Minoan Spiritual Life

A lot of books about the ancient world talk about how there was no separation between religion and daily life back then, how the spirituality of the ancient cultures permeated ordinary life and made all of it sacred. That's every bit as true of the Minoans as it is of the Egyptians, the Babylonians, and other societies of the time. Those same books talk about how this practice is different from the modern world, where many of us go to churches or synagogues or mosques for our religion and don't practice it at home. But the whole spirituality-as-part-of-everyday-life concept isn't as foreign as you might think.

If you're Pagan, regardless of your background or tradition, I bet you have some sort of altar or shrine in your home, maybe even more than one. It might be as simple as a spot on a bookshelf or a fireplace mantel with a figurine and a candle or incense holder next to it. Or it might be a whole shelf or table full of sacred tools, stones, candles, incense, figurines, and other items. But it's there; it's a part of your home and your everyday life. A few lucky people even manage to devote a whole room in their house or apartment to their spiritual pursuits.

Every time you walk past your altar or shrine, you think about the deities and Powers you honor in your spiritual practice. You can perform some sort of devotional every day, or every few days, or only on special occasions that are particularly sacred to you. These are activities you do at home, without having to go to a special building somewhere else to practice your spirituality. They're a part of your everyday life.

The Minoans also had home shrines, lots of them. The simplest ones consisted of a few seashells and maybe an incense dish or a bowl to hold food offerings. Fancier ones included figurines, pitchers (rhytons), offering stands, stones, and other objects. We don't know whether there were formal rules for how to arrange the items on the altars, the way there are in some modern Pagan traditions. Some people may have followed a formal practice, and some may simply have done whatever they felt inspired to do with their home shrines. And just like you and me, the Minoans walked past these altars every day during their ordinary lives. With each passing, they thought about their goddesses and gods and what those deities meant to them.

Fig. 2: Shrine of the Double Axes, Knossos

Just like many Pagans today, some people in ancient Crete devoted whole rooms to their spiritual practice, turning them into large home shrines. Some of these shrine rooms had the walls decorated with fresco murals depicting scenes from nature and myth. They also included large altar tables and other furniture as well as figurines, dishes, labryses, sacred horns, and offering stands. While the small tabletop home altars were probably used by just a single person, I can imagine a whole family gathering in one of the Minoan shrine rooms to do a private ritual honoring their favorite deities.

These are ways the Minoans worshiped and practiced their spirituality at home. But they also went to other places—cave shrines, peak sanctuaries, and the big temple complexes—for special occasions. There, they became part of a larger group, a community celebrating the sacred times together.

Just like all the other cultures of their time, the Minoans had a sacred calendar that punctuated the year with special occasions, breaking up the long stretches of everyday labor with celebrations. The religious calendar for Modern Minoan Paganism has its own chapter later in this book (Chapter 4), but for now let's look at the idea in general. It isn't such a strange concept, really. Our modern secular society has its own set of special occasions— federal holidays, bank holidays, and so on—and each religious tradition has its own set of holy days that its followers observe.

What did the ancient Minoans do for those holy days? Things I think you'll find familiar. They decorated their houses and cooked special foods. They went to public festivals. They attended big rituals with their friends and made special trips to sacred sites. These are activities that many modern Pagans do as well. We have special days when we get together with family and friends to celebrate the turning of the seasons and the times that are sacred for the gods and goddesses we honor, just like the ancient Minoans did.

Like many modern Pagans, the Minoans felt very connected with nature. They revered special spots on their island and visited them to honor certain deities. For instance, several caves in the mountains of Crete were (and still are) sacred to the goddess Rhea. People would make special pilgrimages to these caves on Rhea's special days and probably also at other times if they felt they needed her help. Near Knossos there's a cave that the Minoans dedicated to the midwife-goddess Eileithyia. Pregnant women would visit it to ask a blessing from the goddess for a safe and easy delivery and a healthy baby. This cave was so important to the people of Crete that it was in use from the Neolithic era until the 5th century CE.

When the Minoans went to these cave shrines, they took offerings for the gods—food and drink, figurines, jewelry, and other small items. They left some of the offerings on the altars that were built within the caves, but more often, they threw the offerings into underground pools of water or into deep clefts within the caves. Tossing the offerings into the water and the crevices was a way of sending them to the Underworld, where certain deities and the Ancestors dwelled.

In the cave shrines, we look down toward the Underworld. But what about on the mountaintops? People have thought of the tops of mountains as the abode of the gods for ages. The Minoans followed in this tradition, devoting peak sanctuaries across Crete to their deities of the Sun and Moon, among others. The cave shrines had altars and other small structures built inside them or at the entrances to the caves. But the peak sanctuaries included entire buildings, sometimes very large ones. These buildings housed the clergy who worked at the peak sanctuaries and included ritual rooms as well as outdoor plazas where people gathered for bonfires and ceremonies.

Of course, the people brought offerings to the peak sanctuaries. And where there were large crevices in the mountaintops, the people threw their offerings in as a way of sending them to the gods, just like they did in the cave shrines. We don't know for certain which deities were honored at each of the three dozen or more peak sanctuaries across ancient Crete, but the alignment of the buildings with sunrise and moonrise locations on the eastern horizon tells us that at least the Sun and Moon were vital parts of the worship there.

While the cave shrines were probably used year round, the peak sanctuaries were inaccessible during the winter due to snow and ice. Though the winters on Crete are generally mild, especially near the coast, the tall mountains in the center of the island are topped with snow, and it's freezing up there for several months each year. People simply couldn't make it up the mountain paths after the winter really set in. But there were places the people could go year round, regardless of the weather.

One place that was easy to get to in every large Minoan city was the temple complex. In fact, it's these sprawling, multi-story buildings that made ancient Crete so famous when they were first excavated about a century ago. The temple complexes were home to the priests and priestesses of each city. These people had a lot of work to do to keep their cities running smoothly. They performed public and private rituals, trained the next generation of the clergy, oversaw the farms and orchards the temple owned, supervised the artisans in the temple workshops, and kept track of donations as well as the surplus food that was stored in the temple complexes in case of emergency. The temples appear to have been centers of local government administration, just like the temples in Mesopotamia, as well as religious establishments. And until the Mycenaeans tried to take over Crete, the cities were probably independently governed, even though the whole island shared a common religion and culture.

But just like today, when most people aren't clergy, most people in ancient Crete weren't priests or priestesses. They didn't participate in the ceremonies that took place inside the ritual rooms and in the central courtyards of the temple complexes. In fact, except for a few select lay people, most Minoans never set foot inside the temples. Instead, they participated in the public festivities that took place on the plazas and processional ways just outside the temple walls.

Each temple complex had a large paved plaza along the west side of the building, big enough to hold a crowd. Most of the plazas had broad steps that could act as amphitheater-style seating for the people who gathered there. We can't be sure exactly what kinds of public rituals the temples sponsored, but the art suggests that the Minoan clergy probably put on mystery plays involving singing and dancing in pretty much the same way other ancient cultures did.

These plays acted out the tales of Minoan mythology—the adventures of the gods and goddesses, the creation stories of the Minoan people, and the seasonal legends of the island. Sometimes the plays would be performed entirely on the plaza, possibly on wooden stages built there for that purpose. But there were also broad, paved roads leading up to the temples. They were much fancier than was necessary for ordinary travel. These roads were probably the location of impressive processions at the beginning and ending of public mystery plays and rituals. Everyone loves a good parade, right? There may also have been public feasting on the plazas, with the meals provided by the temple complex using the grain, wine, and other foods they received as donations and offerings. Sharing seems to have been an important facet of Minoan culture.

Fig. 3: Sacred Grove fresco, Knossos

The Minoans oriented their temple complexes and peak sanctuaries toward particular spots on the horizon that marked the rising or setting places of the Sun, Moon, planets, and stars at specific times of the year. These orientations were markers for special times in the Minoan sacred calendar. As far as we know, they didn't use the four directions the way many modern Pagans do, and they didn't associate them with the classical elements of earth, air, fire, and water. Why not? Because that element system was created by the Greeks many centuries after the fall of Minoan civilization. But the Minoans did pay close attention to the heavens and to the Earth around them.

All in all, the ancient Minoans had a wide variety of choices for how to participate in the spiritual traditions of their island. They could focus on their chosen deities in the privacy of their own homes, or travel to sacred places around Crete, or enjoy the performances put on by their local temple complex. To a great extent, we have similar choices today, though obviously the home altar or shrine is the easiest of these to copy in the modern world.

In fact, that's a great place to start: you can set up an altar to a Minoan deity and use that as the focal point for your daily devotions at home. Choose a spot on a table or shelf, or even your dresser, and collect up a few items that make you think of the god or goddess you've chosen. Your altar doesn't have to be fancy; it just needs to have meaning for you. Which deity should you choose? Let's meet the Minoan gods and goddesses, and maybe you'll feel a connection with one of them.

Chapter 2:
Modern Minoan Paganism

The subtitle of this book is *An Introduction to Modern Minoan Paganism*. Modern Minoan Paganism (MMP) is an animist, polytheist tradition of people who feel a connection with the gods and goddesses of Minoan Crete. It's a pathway for modern Pagans to connect with the Minoan deities in a way that makes sense in the 21st century. And MMP is a welcoming tradition, happily open to people of any race, ethnicity, gender or gender identity, sexual orientation, ability level, disability, geographic location, language, education, or socio-economic status. You can find our Official Policies, a list of current board members, and more on our website: ariadnestribe.wordpress.com.

A lot of what we know about ancient Minoan spirituality comes from archaeology, but Modern Minoan Paganism is a revivalist tradition, not a reconstructionist one. Paths like Celtic and Norse Paganism are called 'reconstructionist' because they use historical texts to figure out how the ancient people practiced their spirituality, then they rebuild those practices in the modern world. The thing is, we don't have any texts we can read from the ancient Minoans.

Their own language was recorded in the Linear A script, which still hasn't been deciphered. Toward the end of Minoan times, the Mycenaean Greeks recorded their language in the Linear B script, which is a modified form of Linear A. We can read Linear B, but pretty much all we have that's written in this script is inventory lists, so that doesn't give us much information about anyone's spiritual practices from that time period. We do know the names of a few deities and some priestly titles, but that's about it.

The majority of the written evidence we have comes from many centuries after the fall of Minoan civilization. Long after their towns and temple complexes had crumbled, the Minoans continued to be a source of fascination for the ancient world. Greek and Roman writers wanted to sound like they knew what they were talking about, so they took the few tidbits of folklore and rumor that were still swirling around the Mediterranean and wrote them down as fact. Unfortunately, an awful lot of what we supposedly know about the Minoans comes from these classical sources. In many cases, they're just garbled remnants of Minoan mythology, strongly influenced (and altered) by the misogynistic cultures of later Greece and Rome. In other words, they're not always a reliable source of information about Minoan spiritual beliefs and practices.

So what does that leave us with? In spite of the lack of reliable texts, and in spite of the fact that the towns and temple complexes of ancient Crete were only rediscovered about a century ago, we still have a lot to go on. We have a wide variety of religious images from Minoan art, we know what the Minoans' sacred spaces looked like, and we know who many of their deities are. Dance ethnography and archaeoastronomy have provided some fascinating and vital clues. And we listen to the gods, sharing our experiences with each other to figure out how we can best walk this path together.

This is not a dogmatic tradition. MMP is about developing relationships with the Minoan deities in a way that works for you. Your spiritual practice should add meaning and value to your life, not feel like it's something you have to do just to get it over with. It's also perfectly acceptable to practice MMP alongside any other spiritual tradition, as long as that other tradition doesn't prohibit it.

Modern Minoan Paganism is a living, growing spiritual path that expands as we walk it. Each of us awakens this spirituality in our own lives, learning directly from the gods of ancient Crete.

This book offers you a starting point. Where you go with it is entirely up to you.

Symbols

People are constantly amazed at the naturalistic beauty of Minoan art. But once they catch their breath, the next thing they notice is all the symbols. You're probably familiar with a lot of them: labryses, horns, lilies, griffins, spirals, stars. So what do they all mean, and which ones are used for what purpose?

Each of the gods and goddesses listed in Chapter 3 has their own symbol set. From Ariadne and her labyrinth to the horns of the Minotaur, each of these symbols can help you connect more closely with an aspect of the deity we associate it with. You can find examples of these symbols in Minoan art and artifacts as well as in modern art and jewelry. But what if you're looking for an emblem for Modern Minoan Paganism in general and not for a specific deity? I can offer you a few possibilities.

The Malia Bee Pendant

This is our tradition's official logo: the Malia bee pendant, a small piece of gold jewelry created by a Minoan artisan between 1800 and 1700 BCE. It was found in the tombs of the Chrysolakos cemetery at Malia. This beautiful little pendant is replete with symbolism that has meaning for us as modern Pagans, and that surely had meaning for the ancient people who included it in the burial of their beloved dead.

First and most obvious of all, the pendant features two bees. The honeybee is a vital part of the environment and has been important to humans for ages. In MMP, we associate the bee with the Melissae (check out their details in Chapter 3). But we also remember that bees are social insects: they live in a community, just as we form a community with each other in MMP. The bees hold a drop of honey above a piece of honeycomb, a reminder of the sweetness of our relationship with the divine and with each other.

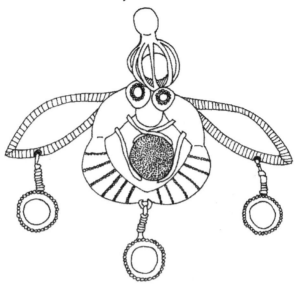

Fig. 4: Gold bee pendant, Malia

Below the bees there are three circular pendants. These remind us of the Three Mothers, the goddesses who are the head of our pantheon and the source from with the other deities unfold. The Three Mothers reflect the three realms that we acknowledge in MMP: the land, the sky, and the sea. The triple pendants also remind us of the many other threes in the pantheon: the three Daughters, the three Young Gods, and the three pairs of Horned Ones. You can find out about all of these deities and more in Chapter 3.

Labrys and Horns

Another prominent symbol in MMP is the labrys-and-horns combination, after which this book is named. This pairing is found all over Minoan art in the frescoes, seals, and fancy goldwork. The versions below and on the book cover use the stylized sacred horns, but this symbol combo can also be found with realistic bovine horns as well.

The labrys-and-horns combination unites multiple layers of both masculine and feminine iconography in a way that reminds us of the egalitarian nature of Minoan religion and society: men and women, gods and goddesses as equals. A variation of this pair, also seen in Minoan art, is the sacred horns with a pillar or column in the center. The pillar or column is a stand-in for the goddess, a stylized and simplified tree, similar to the Asherah pole from the Levant.

There are a lot of different interpretations of the labrys-and-horns combination. Like most religious iconography, it ultimately has multiple layers of meaning and not just a single definition. For me, that's part of what makes symbols magical—they can be more than one thing at a time.

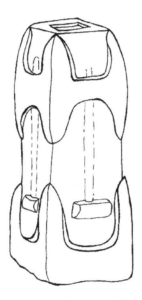

Fig. 5: Limestone labrys and horns, Knossos

The labrys is associated with the sacred feminine because its shape is similar to the vulva (blades = labia). It's also connected with the Earth and the cycles of the seasons, particularly the agricultural cycle, since it's the shape of the hoe-axes the Minoans used to work their fields and that can still be found in rural parts of Crete. On top of that, the labrys can represent the human soul and the concept of reincarnation if you view it as a stylized butterfly, a beautiful creature that undergoes metamorphosis as part of its life cycle. Around the world and across time, the butterfly has long been a symbol of the soul.

In a sense, the labrys can also represent the combination of the masculine and feminine. In Minoan art, we find labrys blades by themselves, butterfly-like, but we also find many labryses with handles or atop poles. The labrys blade is a strongly female symbol, but setting it up on a pole or at the end of a handle suggests the addition of a phallus.

The sacred horns are a well-known emblem of the horned gods: the Minotaur, the Minocapros, and the Minelathos. They can also represent two of the three horned goddesses, Europa and Amalthea, because cows and nanny goats also have horns. All cattle, both male and female, had horns until just over a century ago, when ranchers started polling cattle—removing their horns—to keep them from goring each other in close confines. So you can't necessarily assume a bovine head with horns in Minoan art is a bull; sometimes it's a cow.

The sacred horns can also represent the horizon, like the similar Egyptian *aker* symbol. There are several well-known double-peaked mountains in Crete, and the Minoans considered these mountains sacred. Minoan peak sanctuaries and temples also had the stylized sacred horns on their roofs. We think the Minoans used these natural and artificial sacred horns as horizon markers for watching the rising and setting of the Sun, Moon, planets, and stars between the two peaks. Some of us also view the sacred horns as the place where the goddess births celestial objects into the sky.

So the horns are a doorway between the worlds—the upper (daylight) world and the Underworld. This adds an interesting dimension to their meaning, since spirit journeying appears to have been part of Minoan spiritual practice, and a lot of Minoan deities have shamanic characteristics.

Taken together, the labrys and horns embody a wide range of meanings that give us a vivid snapshot of the Minoan belief system: masculine and feminine in balance; the Upperworld and the Underworld as two parts of the whole; doorways and cycles and metamorphosis moving in a circle or spiral rather than a straight line.

The Snake Goddess

Another well-known symbol of ancient Minoan culture and religion is this Snake Goddess figurine from Knossos. There's a lot of controversy over who or what she actually represents and whether she has been reconstructed accurately. Even Sir Arthur Evans wavered as to whether she was a votary (a worshiper or priestess) or a goddess. But I think we can all agree she's an icon of ancient Crete. Some people see her as a goddess whose form includes the Serpent Mother. She could also be a priestess performing a ritual, drawing down the Snake Goddess.

Fig. 6: Faience Snake Goddess figurine, Knossos

However you view this fascinating artifact, she brings ancient Minoan society and spirituality into the modern world in a very real way. Here is a real woman taking a central role in a spiritual tradition that goes all the way back to the Bronze Age. This is no shrinking violet, and I doubt anyone sees her as submissive or weak.

This is one of two women-with-snakes figurines that Sir Arthur Evans' team found at Knossos. There are also several snake-goddess figurine forgeries that have shown up in museums over the years. If nothing else, the forgeries show just how popular the snake goddess is as a symbol of Minoan religion—every museum wanted one. The 'snake goddess' type of figurine, and whatever kind of religious practice she represented, lasted several centuries beyond the end of Minoan civilization on Crete. We know this because of a post-Minoan-era terracotta goddess figurine (one of the kind that have a bell-jar shaped skirt) who's holding snakes in her upraised hands and whose hair looks like writhing snakes.

The Sacral Scarf

Another interesting symbol that's found throughout Minoan art but that isn't quite as well-known as the others is called the sacral scarf. This is not the same as the *tyet* knot associated with Isis in ancient Egyptian religion, which is a short length of cord formed into a particular type of looped knot. Instead, the Minoan sacral scarf is a length of woven fabric, fringed on the ends and looped around into a distinctive shape.

The sacral scarf comes from a unique Minoan practice: the worshiping of the priestess' clothes after a ritual. The people who served as priests and priestesses in ancient Crete took part in rituals that involved trance possession. In other words, the gods and goddesses descended into the priests and priestesses during the rites. So a priestess would be considered the goddess incarnate during a ritual, and the clothes she was wearing would have been literally touched by the goddess. After the ritual, her clothes were hung up on special stands where people could worship them; the clothes hanging on these stands are shown on some seals from Minoan Crete.

Fig. 7: Sacral scarf fresco, Nirou Khani

It's possible that people came to touch the clothes and ask for healing and other kinds of help from the goddess. We don't have any evidence of the priest's clothes being worshiped in this way, but it's certainly possible that happened as well. Future archaeological discoveries may give us more clues about this interesting practice.

The sacral scarf represents the healing and helping presence of the goddess in the clothing even after the goddess has 'flown' at the end of a ritual. It also represents being touched by the divine, either directly or indirectly. We find images of the sacral scarf on Minoan seals and frescoes. The people of ancient Crete also made little plaster replicas of the sacral scarf which were hung up in people's homes or placed in their graves.

Practices

MMP is a formal tradition with members and chapters, but you don't have to be an official member to follow our practices and connect with the Minoan deities. Both solitaries and groups can practice MMP. We have a standard ritual format that works for everything from a simple devotional at your home altar to a large public group ritual; more about those in Chapters 5 and 6. MMP is suitable both for people who are new to Paganism and for those who already have some experience in other traditions or on their own unique path. We're not an exclusionary tradition. You're welcome to practice MMP alongside any other tradition, as long as the other tradition doesn't have any rules against it.

If you're new to MMP, begin with our three mother goddesses — they're the core of our pantheon. You can find out more about them and all the others in Chapter 3. Over time, it's likely that one or two other deities will eventually make their presence known to you, and you can build a relationship with them from that point onward. There was probably a wide variety of individual spiritual practice in ancient Crete, since so many people had household shrines and altars.

Speaking of altars, a good place to start is to set one up. Chapter 5 can help you do this. Creating an altar or shrine is worth your time because it anchors your spirituality in the material world and gives you a focus for devotionals, rituals, and meditations. Just seeing it as you walk past will 'key in' your Minoan spirituality and help keep it fresh in your mind. Personally, I find my home altars to be comforting, like I have the gods keeping watch over me every day.

You'll need to decide what kind of spiritual practice makes the most sense for you and how often you can reasonably do whatever you're going to do. Devotionals and prayers are a good place to start. They're simple and don't require anything more than your time and attention. Offerings are another option, by themselves or as part of more involved rituals. A full ritual, using the standard format, is probably not something you want to do every day, since it takes some time to prepare and enact. But you don't have to perform a whole ritual to simply say a devotional or make an offering.

Figure out how much time your proposed spiritual practice is going to take, and then be honest with yourself about whether you actually have that much time to devote regularly. Sometimes simple is better, if it means the difference between getting in there and doing it or not getting around to it. I know it's tempting to Do It All, but starting slow is a better choice, because you're more likely to keep up a simple practice than a complicated one.

Many people like to meditate on whatever issues come up in their lives and ask the gods for guidance. You can even request that the deities help you figure out what your spiritual practice should include. It takes some work to learn to listen, and it's always a good idea to remember that your life choices are still yours to make, no matter what you experience in your meditations. But regular meditation, whether you're asking for help or simply focusing or blanking your mind, is a useful spiritual practice that can have a positive impact on the rest of your life.

One thing that happens to a lot of us as we explore spiritual paths is that we start out with all kinds of enthusiasm, saying devotionals and making offerings every day. Then life gets busy, emergencies happen, and that daily practice falls by the wayside. This is especially true for solitaries, who don't have scheduled group events to keep them on track, but it's also true for people who belong to groups. Don't panic—these things happen. Be sure to apologize to the gods if you had promised you would approach them regularly, but also remember to cut yourself some slack. You're a human being with a modern life to deal with. So take a deep breath and get back to it. The gods will remember you, and you can pick up where you left off (though if it's been a really long time, a generous offering is a nice gesture).

Chapter 3:
The Pantheon

Even if you haven't researched Minoan spirituality, you've probably heard of Ariadne, Dionysus, and the Minotaur. The names of Rhea and Amalthea might also be familiar. Even though the Minoans lived thousands of years ago, their spirituality has threaded its way through the centuries, intertwining with later pantheons and inspiring artists, writers, and poets all the way up to now.

A lot of the Minoan gods and goddesses were incorporated into the Greek pantheon centuries after the fall of Minoan civilization, so it can be hard to tell exactly what they were like to start with. The Greek versions of the Minoan deities held onto some of their earlier characteristics, but they also made changes— sometimes major ones—in their stories and even their identities. For many people, the only versions they've ever heard are the Greek myths, which aren't very flattering toward the Minoan deities. It takes a little digging, but eventually the gods' and goddesses' original personalities shine through, and we can connect with the way we think they existed on Crete during the heyday of Minoan civilization.

One interesting feature of the Minoan pantheon is that it doesn't fit into a tidy, human-style family tree. Many Pagan pantheons—Celtic, Norse, and Greek among them—are shown as family trees, with the relationships among all the gods and goddesses just like your relationship with your parents, grandparents, siblings, cousins, and so forth. But it's not always easy to figure out how the Minoan deities are related to each other. For instance, the goat-goddess Amalthea is referred to in different myths as Rhea's sister, her twin, and her alter ego. Which is it? Or is it all three? Ariadne is called Rhea's daughter as well as her alter ego. Instead of just one mother goddess, there are three—or maybe four, depending on how you look at it. And they have daughters and sons in a way that's not remotely human. Then we have the Horned Ones—the Minotaur and Europa, the Minocapros and Amalthea, the Minelathos and Britomartis—who look an awful lot like each other, just in the form of different animals. Instead of a family tree, it looks more like a tangled web, or maybe a carnival fun house full of mirrors.

This "fun house" effect comes from the micro-pantheons among the gods and goddesses. A micro-pantheon is a small group of deities who have their own set of stand-alone mythos and celebrations. Multiple micro-pantheons join together to create the overall set of myths. This was a typical way for deities to be arranged prior to the Iron Age, and personally, I find it fascinating. Some micro-pantheons survived the Iron Age shift to mega-pantheons (the type with a single powerful male god at the top), though many of them slowly faded out over time. Some examples you might be familiar with are the Egyptian trio of Isis, Set, and Horus, or the pairs Attis and Cybele or Artemis and Hekate. The Mysteries, in their Minoan version with Ariadne and Rhea or their pre-Greek mainland version with Persephone and Demeter (before the addition of Hades and Zeus to the story) also count as micro-pantheons. So look for these little "short story sets" within the larger scope of the mythology.

Another aspect of the Minoan gods and goddesses is something you may have encountered in other pantheons: multiple epithets for each deity. So besides their "official" name, any given god or goddess has what you might call sacred nicknames. These may refer to their attributes (one of Therasia's epithets is Kalliste, meaning "beautiful") or their roles in religion and myth (Ariadne is Lady of the Labyrinth). You'll find each deity's epithets in their individual listing below.

In addition to the "big name" gods and goddesses we're familiar with, the Minoans revered a wide variety of nature spirits. While some plants and animals were directly associated with deities (cattle with the Horned Ones and lilies with Ariadne, for instance), many features of the natural landscape had their own local spirits, from the sacred mountains to rivers and creeks and even trees. We don't know for sure what names the Minoans called them, so we have to use later Greek and other terms for some. Collectively, we can simply call them nature spirits. But they all reflect the Minoans' animistic view of the world: everything is alive, and everything has a spirit.

The rivers and creeks across Crete were the homes of the fresh-water naiads, while the salt-water nereids frolicked in the waves along the island's shore. Dryads animated the trees around the island. The forests of Crete held the spirits of animals, plants, and even stones and wind. The spirits of the wind are still important in folklore around the Mediterranean. There were nature spirits of the mountains on Crete, usually named for each sacred mountain. For instance, Mt. Ida was home to the Idaeae. These were separate from the Goddess herself, who embodied the mountain as part of Mother Earth. Like so many ancient cultures, the Minoans saw life and sacredness in the world around them and chose to focus on those nature spirits and do them reverence.

Unless you happen to live in Crete, you're not likely to encounter the nature spirits of the Minoan world. But since MMP is an Earth-oriented spirituality, you can honor the nature spirits wherever you live. That's exactly what the Minoans did. And you can bet they made offerings to the local nature spirits wherever they traveled. So make friends with your local trees and rivers, and remember the Minoans when you do.

In Chapter 5, you'll have the opportunity to undertake a ritual to connect with the Minoan deities. I'll also show you how to set up and consecrate an altar you can use to honor them. In this chapter, each deity's entry includes details about their characteristics as well as suggestions for items to use when you set up an altar to them. You'll also learn which offerings and divination methods we've found them to prefer, and how best to present yourself if you'll be embodying them in ritual. You can find out more about the concept of embodying a deity in Chapter 5. But right now, let's meet the gods and goddesses of ancient Crete.

The Mothers and Their Children

In a matrilineal society, ancestry is traced through the mother. Fathers are still there, of course. Men aren't irrelevant, and they aren't treated as badly as women often have been in many patrilineal societies. But the family line traces through the women. And since mythos reflects culture, the Minoan pantheon begins with the mother. In Modern Minoan Paganism, we have three mother goddesses. You'll find the number three turning up over and over again as a major sacred symbol.

Before we go any further, though, let's talk about a concept you've probably already heard of: the goddess in three aspects as the Maiden, Mother, and Crone. This is not a structure that we use in MMP, because it's a fairly modern invention. The British writer Robert Graves created the idea of the threefold goddess in Maiden/Mother/Crone format in the mid-20th century and popularized it in his book *The White Goddess*. Now, Grave's concept of the threefold goddess has a lot of meaning for a lot of Pagans. It's a perfectly valid way to approach the divine feminine. But it's not historical, and it most certainly doesn't go back all the way to the Minoans. So what do we use instead?

There are a lot of threes in our pantheon, but if you look closely, there are also lots of dualities. In particular, the pairing of an older goddess with a younger goddess (any of the Three Mothers with their daughters) or a younger god with an older one (Korydallos with Daedalus) appear to be quite ancient, going back at least to the Neolithic. In MMP we consider this younger/elder duality to reflect into the human sphere as well, just like the Maiden/Mother/Crone triplicity does. To express this idea in our own lives, we've come up with three sets of paired terms that can be applied to both deities and humans:

Feminine: Maiden and Matriarch
Masculine: Stripling and Sage
Gender-Neutral: Youth and Elder

The younger terms apply to the first half of a person's life, when they're still figuring out who they are and how they want to live their life. The older terms apply to the second half of a person's life, when they've come into their own and begun to be comfortable with their own power. These terms can be used to help an individual relate to the deities in our pantheon, and the transition from younger to elder can be acknowledge with a rite of passage. But we're talking specifically about our pantheon in this chapter, so let's get back to the deities in question.

As I noted above, the Minoan pantheon doesn't shake out neatly into a human-style family tree. But we do have what you might call mothers and their children, so we'll start there. I'll begin with some deity names and their relationships with each other, and you can read about them in more detail in their individual listings further down.

The Three Mothers, or the Three, are the goddesses Rhea, Therasia, and Posidaeja. They rule and embody the three realms of land, sky, and sea. Each one of them has a daughter and a son in the Modern Minoan pantheon. So the three triplicities look like this:

Land: Rhea — Ariadne — Tauros Asterion
Sky: Therasia — Arachne — Korydallos
Sea: Posidaeja — Antheia — Dionysus

Each trio is made up of one of the mother goddesses with her children, one daughter and one son each. These deities all have their own characteristics and responsibilities, but they're also interrelated. So the Mothers are a trio, as are the Daughters and the Young Gods. We can consider the three Young Gods to be brothers and the three Daughters to be sisters, even though they have three different mothers (I told you the Minoan pantheon doesn't fit neatly into a human-style family tree!). These smaller groups could be considered micro-pantheons, and as you can see, some deities belong to more than one group.

The Three Mothers have a trio of winged creatures that we associate with them: doves with Rhea, swallows with Therasia, and flying fish with Posidaeja. Wings put them above the realm of humanity, above the normal and into the numinous.

The Mothers are the base or core of the pantheon. In our standard ritual format, we call on them regardless of which other deities we're inviting in any given ritual. We can choose to focus on one or all three of the Mothers in rituals and devotionals. The same goes for the Young Gods and the Daughters: we can address them individually or as a group. Let's discover the details about these gods and goddesses, and all the others in our pantheon.

Rhea

Pronunciation: REE-ah or RAY-ah

Epithets: Ida (ee-DAH), Earth-Mother, Mountain-Mother, Island-Mother, Mother of the Dark Earth, Grain-Mother, Lady of the Doves

Many ancient people thought of the Earth where they lived as a goddess. The Minoans were no different. To them, the island of Crete was their Earth Mother goddess Rhea. Envisioning the island itself as a goddess embodied in the sand, soil, and mountains made their home sacred. If the Earth itself (herself) is divine, then we have a greater obligation to take good care of it (her). This is one very important idea we can bring forward into the modern world, to make the places where we live sacred again. Though she is Minoan, Rhea can help us connect with the Earth wherever we happen to be.

Even though Rhea eventually became part of the classical Greek pantheon, she was originally from Crete, and Greek mythology reflects this fact. The Greek myths talk about how Rhea gave birth to her divine son in a cave on Crete. There are several caves on Crete that were supposedly *the* sacred cave of Rhea, but two of them are more famous than the others. One is on a mountain that's now called Mt. Psiloritis but that was originally called Mt. Ida. It's the Idaean cave, and its name gives us one of Rhea's epithets. The second cave is on Mt. Dikte and is called the Psychro cave. Both of these caves were popular pilgrimage sites during Minoan times.

Now, the Greeks said the baby that Rhea birthed in her sacred cave was their god Zeus, but the original story involves a Minoan deity. We think the divine child born in Rhea's cave at Midwinter may originally have been Tauros Asterion—he does seem to be "earthier" than Dionysus—or possibly even Korydallos, since one of the oldest Eurasian myth cycles involves the Sun goddess rebirthing herself in a cave at Winter Solstice. But the Greeks just loved Dionysus, calling him Cretan Zeus and insisting that he had to be at the top of the Minoan pantheon. So he's the one who ended up in the story that made it through the centuries in garbled and fragmented form. You can have a look at the section about Dionysus below to learn more about his birth story.

Rhea's main function in the Minoan pantheon is as a mother, both the mother of Dionysus, to whom she gives birth each year at the Winter Solstice, and the mother of all life on Crete—plant, animal, and human, including the grain crops. By the time of the big towns and temple complexes, the Minoans probably thought of Rhea as a symbolic mother, but in earlier times, the people of Crete may have considered her to be their actual ancestor. Most pantheons around the world grew out of ancestor worship, and the Minoans were surely no different. If your family had lived in the same place for more generations than anyone could remember, you might think the land was your great-great-grandmother, too.

Like the other sacred caves, these were places where people made offerings. But what stands out about the Idaean and Psychro caves is that they're the only two Minoan-era cave shrines where people offered figurines in human form. All the other cave shrines had offerings of jewelry, tiny labryses, small items like pins and tweezers, and knives. In other words, items people probably had in their homes. But for making offerings at Rhea's caves, people went out and bought special bronze and terracotta figurines in the shape of human beings. These little statues probably represented the people making the offerings or the people they wanted Rhea to help. I can see a woman making an offering of a male statue and asking Rhea to help her brother recover from an injury. Or giving a statue that represented herself as thanks for some happy occasion.

One interesting aspect of Rhea's story is that she had a group of nine attendants, the Kouretes, who guarded her cave, especially when her divine child was there. They were known for their rhythmic chanting, drumming, and dancing. While we know them as mythological figures, they may also have been human priests of Rhea at her cave shrines on Crete. They may also have been associated with Dionysus, Rhea's son, since he was called 'the greatest kouros,' or possibly with Tauros Asterion or Korydallos, all of whom are divine son figures and hence youthful gods. The Greek word *kouros* means youth or boy, and Kouretes comes from the same word root as kouros.

Besides mountains and caves, Rhea was also associated with the pithoi (that's the plural—the singular is pithos), the huge pottery jars in which the Minoans stored oil, wine, and other food and sometimes buried their dead. In other words, Rhea's pithos was the source of sustenance and the womb-symbol to which everyone returned after death. In MMP we consider Rhea, the Mountain-Mother, to be the divine patron of potters. More about that in the listing for the Daktyls and Hekaterides further down in this chapter.

One of Rhea's titles was Pandora, which means 'all-giver.' If you've read any Greek mythology, you know the story of Pandora opening a box and letting all the bad things out into the world, with only hope left over to redeem her terrible action. Like so many other Minoan deities (Ariadne and the Minotaur come to mind here), Rhea Pandora was mocked and belittled by the Greeks in order to make their own culture look advanced and to portray the Minoans as primitive by comparison. But if we dig underneath the cultural spin the Greeks put on Rhea Pandora, it looks like her pithos (not a box, but a large vase) originally contained everything, both good and bad, like the bottomless cauldrons in Celtic mythology. Interestingly, the Minoans used pithoi not just to store their staple foods (grain, wine, and olive oil) but also to bury their dead, a symbolic return to the Great Mother's womb. So we find the Great Mother who is the All-Giver, the Source of All, who sustains and renews life and provides comfort in death.

In addition to the pithos, Rhea has some other symbols in MMP. As a mother goddess, we associate her with the Asiatic lily (*Lilium* species). The double-curl that Minoan artists used when they depicted the lily is breast-symbolic, and was sometimes extravagantly exaggerated and stylized. In Minoan art, lilies are most commonly painted in white and red, but they may have been grown in a wide variety of colors. We also connect the lily with Rhea's daughter Ariadne; you'll find those details in Ariadne's listing further down in this chapter.

We also associate Rhea with doves, ground birds that show up repeatedly in Minoan art. Several species of these gentle birds are native to the Mediterranean. Along with doves, we consider cypress trees to belong to Rhea. The ancient Greek writer Diodorus Siculus said there was a cypress grove dedicated to her at Knossos. So cypress trees are Rhea's, and so is cypress wood, which can be found in some kinds of incense. Poppies also belong to her, but they belong to her daughter Ariadne as well. Since the early days of agriculture, poppies have grown in the grain fields alongside the wheat and barley. The Minoans produced opium, using it probably for medicine as well as for ritual hallucinogenic purposes. In MMP we view the poppy as Rhea's gift to her daughter.

Rhea also shows up in Minoan iconography with lions. This symbol set may go back to Neolithic Anatolia, where we find lions in the sacred art, including one figurine of a goddess on a lion throne. So a pair of lions on a Minoan seal, flanking a pillar or column (a symbol of the goddess) tells us we're looking at a reference to Rhea.

If you'd like to create an altar to Rhea, you can use her title 'Earth Mother' as a clue for what kinds of items to include. Anything that makes you think of the Earth is a good choice: stones in shades of green and brown; leaves, twigs, and other natural objects you've gathered from outdoors; fresh flowers or a potted plant. There are plenty of Earth Goddess statues available, both online and in local metaphysical shops. Since the dove is also Rhea's symbol, a figurine or image of a dove could represent her on your altar.

If you'd like to focus on her Grain-Mother aspect, you could opt for a Snake Goddess figurine; snakes eat the rodents that eat the grain, so they're sacred to the grain goddess. Or you could choose a figurine that shows a woman holding a sheaf of grain— yes, you can repurpose a Demeter or Ceres statue for this, as long as it hasn't been consecrated to another goddess already and doesn't have the other goddess' name painted or embossed on it. Or you could simply set some stalks of wheat or barley on your altar.

You could use an altar cloth in any earthy-toned natural fabric or leave a wooden tabletop bare as the base so you can see the wood grain under your altar decorations. I like to set up my altar to Rhea outside, where the fresh air and sunshine will bless it. To me, that seems an appropriate way to honor her. But indoor altars also work well, and we don't all have access to private outdoor spaces.

When you want to make an offering to Rhea, milk of almost any sort (cow, goat, even non-dairy ones like soy, oat, or almond milk) is always a safe bet, though she isn't too keen on coconut milk, we've found. Grain is also a good choice, either plain (wheat berries, for instance) or in bread. The Minoans had three different kinds of wheat, including emmer wheat, plus barley and rye, so those should be your first choices. For offerings, homemade bread is always your best option, but a good quality purchased loaf will also work. And no, you don't have to offer the whole loaf, just a slice or two. Rhea will also usually accept fresh fruit in the varieties that were grown in ancient Crete: figs, dates, grapes, quinces (but not pomegranates—they're for Underworld deities and the spirits of the dead). Some people can offer her wine, but she doesn't always like it. She seems to like white wine better than red. Interestingly, she also enjoys offerings of wool, especially unspun and otherwise unprocessed (unscoured, for those of you who are into the fiber arts). If you can get some fresh fleece from a farmer or a spinning and weaving supply shop, that's your best choice. You can offer it alone or in combination with other offerings. Wool plus sheep's milk is a powerful offering to her. Like the other two Great Mothers, Rhea will always accept offerings of honey.

For divination with Rhea as your guide, choose a natural, earthy substance: a handful of stones tossed onto the ground will make patterns you can interpret, as will a bunch of leaves. You can ask Rhea for signs about a particular matter when you're outdoors, then keep an eye out for anything unusual, especially on the ground and among the trees. You can also scry in wood grain, believe it or not. Find a piece of wood with some interesting grain marks on it (lots of lines plus some knots). Use it as your meditative focus, preferably in low light like the dappled sunlight of the forest or the soft light of a candle.

For embodying her in ritual, keep in mind that you're representing an Earth goddess. Your clothing should be made of natural fibers, in colors that will depend on the focus of your ritual. The Grain-Mother might wear the colors of autumn harvest and carry stalks of wheat or barley. If you want to embody Rhea simply as an Earth goddess, choose colors in shades of green and brown that evoke the natural world. If you really want to go all out, make sure all your fabric was colored with natural dyes.

Therasia

Pronunciation: tehr-AH-see-ya

Epithets: *Kalliste (kah-LISS-tay, "the Beautiful"), Khelidon (kheh-lee-DON, "the Swallow"), Sun-Mother, Fire-Mother, Fire of Heaven*

Though many people are used to the Sun in the guise of a god, in the Mediterranean we find a very old Sun goddess instead. In MMP, we call her Therasia. She represents the sky portion of the great triplicity and is the apportioner of the solar year. As the Sun, she grows in power over the course of the year until she's at her greatest height at the Summer Solstice. This is when she beats down over the Mediterranean, heating everything up until much of Crete is crispy-brown and dry. From that point, she slowly shifts back down, a bit at a time, until she reaches her lowest, dimmest point at the Winter Solstice. At Midwinter, it's almost like she dies, or maybe retreats into a cave for a short while. Then, like other Sun goddesses have done since time immemorial, she rebirths herself and begins the yearly process once again.

It's possible that the caves the Mycenaeans recorded as being the place where Rhea gave birth to a divine child at Winter Solstice were originally symbolic of the cave where the Sun goddess dies and is reborn at that point in the year. Across Eurasia, the old Sun goddess is said to retreat to a cave at Midwinter. Western Anatolia, where the Minoans' ancestors came from during the Neolithic, is full of hills and caves. So it's possible the concept of caves as sacred sites associated with the Sun goes back that far.

In addition to the Sun and its light, Therasia also rules volcanoes and hot springs, as do many other Eurasian Sun goddesses. Ancient people thought of the Sun as traveling beneath the Earth at night, from west to east. From this point of view developed the idea that, while the Sun is "below," it (she) heats up the water in the springs and the lava in the volcanoes. The volcanic island of Thera (modern name = Santorini) was sacred to her, and the name we call her by now, Therasia, is also the name of one of the small islands that remained after the volcano erupted during the Bronze Age.

Therasia's symbols are the date palm tree and its fruit as well as the griffin, a mythical creature with the body of a lion and the head and wings of an eagle. The famous murex dye with its blood-red to deep purple color is also hers. The Minoans produced the rare murex dye centuries before it became famous as Phoenician purple; it takes thousands of murex sea snails to produce a single gram of dye. Another dyestuff, this time in the form of a flower, is also sacred to Therasia: saffron. The blood-red stamens of the saffron crocus dye a deep, sunny yellow, giving us Therasia's two sacred colors: red and gold. In MMP we consider Therasia to be the divine patron of pre-Iron-Age metalsmiths (those who work with bronze and precious metals). Though the ore for metalsmithing comes from the Earth, it's Therasia's gift of fire that allows us to transform it into attractive and useful metal objects. More about this in the section about the Daktyls and Hekaterides further down in this chapter. In MMP we consider metal instruments like gongs and cymbals to belong to Therasia, and we don't use them when honoring other deities.

Therasia is particular about sharing altar space with other deities. She's willing to share with the other two Great Mothers (Rhea and Posidaeja) as well as with her son, Korydallos and her daughter, Arachne. But she isn't too keen on sharing with other deities except for the brief time when she and the other two Great Mothers are represented on the altar along with any other deities being honored in the standard MMP ritual format (the format is given in detail in Chapter 5). If you want to set up an altar to her that will stay up for the long term, I recommend dedicating it just to her. It doesn't have to be large or elaborate, but it should be hers and hers alone. Please note, this doesn't mean you have to work only with Therasia and no other deities. The Minoan deities aren't the jealous type. It just means that Therasia demands her own space if you're going to include her in your spiritual practice.

Ideally, an altar to Therasia will be located somewhere the sunlight can touch it, such as near a window. Blood red and sunny yellow are her colors, and anything shiny or sparkly, especially in golden or bronze tones, can evoke her. Mirrors are also Therasia's provenance. The Minoans didn't have silvered glass mirrors like we do; theirs were made of polished bronze. If you can find sheet bronze at a craft shop, a round of it makes an excellent mirror for an altar to Therasia. But a plain round modern mirror also works; round is always better than square or rectangular for this purpose, though an octagonal mirror will work all right. Keep mirrors covered with a soft cloth when you're not actively working with the altar (making an offering, praying or meditating, performing a ritual). You're not likely to find Sun goddess statues in most metaphysical shops, but if you find a plain figurine (without any of the symbols of another deity) you can paint it with metallic gold or, preferably, shiny bronze paint and it will work well.

As a Sun goddess, Therasia enjoys offerings of fire in its many forms. Her strongest preference is for full-blown wood fires: bonfires, campfires, a roaring fire in your fireplace. She also likes those wood-wick candles that crackle like a campfire, but otherwise she seems to prefer oil lamps to candles (the Minoans didn't have candles—they hadn't been invented yet). She also likes fiery scents; frankincense is a good choice for incense. Though fiery spices like cinnamon and ginger were unknown in ancient Crete, Therasia does seem to like them in the form of incense and essential oil. She doesn't like hot peppers, though. She's also happy to receive offerings of the two fruits that we associate with her: dates and quinces. If you're looking to give her a libation, she enjoys retsina (resinated wine, which has been made on Crete since Minoan times). She's also the only one of our deities who likes offerings of hard liquor, preferably the amber-colored ones (whiskey, rum, Scotch).

The most obvious method of divination to do with Therasia as your guide is scrying in flame. A single candle flame in a darkened room is an easy option for most people. But if you have a fireplace or will be in the vicinity of a campfire or bonfire, you could try scrying in those as well. If you want to get fancy with some fire-themed divination, you can write your question or issue on a piece of paper, burn it (in a fireplace or fireproof container, please) then read the ashes for images or patterns. With Therasia's aid you can also scry in mirrors—not black ones, but bright mirrors, preferably bronze or golden in color, but silver ones will also work. You can also scry in a water-mirror: the reflection of the midday Sun in a still bowl of water. And you can read the patterns of sunlight that moving water reflects onto nearby surfaces like walls.

If you'll be embodying Therasia in ritual, consider wearing clothing that's shiny or sparkly, in shades of gold and bronze, as well as metallic or glittery makeup. You want people to think of sunlight and bright shining things when they see you. Therasia isn't as particular as some other Minoan deities about the use of natural fibers; she's often more interested in the effect the outfit has on onlookers than on the content of the materials. So gather up some garments that give the impression of a bright shining being, and glimmer and gleam your way into the ritual.

Posidaeja

Pronunciation: poe-see-DYE-ah
Epithets: Thalassa (tah-LAH-sah or tha-LAH-sah, "the sea"), Water-
Mother, Grandmother Ocean, Mother of the Waters.
Posidaeja is an ocean goddess with a name so old that it appears on the Linear B tablets. It's Posidaeja's name that the Greeks appear to have altered for their own ocean deity, Poseidon. Crete's an island, and many of the Minoans made their living from the sea, either fishing or trading. It makes sense that they would have a deity who embodied the water that cradled their island and over whose depths they sailed to fish and trade. I suspect they also thanked her for the special bounty of food from the sea that sustained them when their land-based food sources weren't doing so well, like during droughts or after earthquakes and tidal waves.

The Minoans were fond of the sea that surrounded their home. This shows in their art and the items they collected up for their shrines. Beautiful images of flying fish, squid, octopuses, coral, seaweed and other sea life adorn their frescoes and pottery. Archaeologists have dug up lots of real seashells as well as man-made terracotta and carved stone versions that the Minoans displayed on their altars and shrines. They even turned triton shells into musical instruments, trumpets that sounded a deep, echoing tone at ritual time.

Though the Minoans focused on the Mediterranean Sea that surrounds Crete, Posidaeja works as an ocean goddess in general, wherever you happen to live. After all, if you look at a map, there really is only one ocean; it's all connected. I suspect the Minoans understood that fact, since we know they sailed out into the Atlantic Ocean and possibly along the western coast of India as well. And ultimately, Posidaeja is the goddess of all the water on Earth, since it's all part of a single environmental and atmospheric cycle. If you're inland, you can connect with her via any sort of water. Though natural bodies of water (rivers, ponds, lakes, streams) are more evocative, a simple bowl of water will also work.

To set up an altar to Posidaeja, begin with shades of blue and aqua as well as shimmery surfaces like silver mirrors and shiny fabrics that suggest the feeling of water. You can include any of the usual ocean-themed creatures and images: seashells, fish, dolphins, flying fish, octopuses, squid, seaweed, and ocean waves. In MMP, the octopus (including the paper nautilus a.k.a. argonaut) is a special symbol of Therasia. The Minoan art that depicts sea creatures is especially appropriate, but photos and artwork in other styles can still evoke Grandmother Ocean. You could even fill a small bowl with salt water—or actual sea-water, if you have access to the ocean.

If you don't have a natural affinity for the ocean (some of us are what you might call "mountain people" rather than "beach people") you might find you can connect with her better via the image of a sea turtle. Though sea turtles don't show up in the Minoan art that has been found so far, they're native to the Mediterranean. Loggerhead sea turtles nest on Crete and lay their eggs on the island's beaches. Green and leatherback sea turtles also swim the seas around Crete. So try out the image of Posidaeja as a sea turtle if the octopus isn't working for you.

If you have a triton or conch shell, either a natural one or a replica, this is an excellent addition to an altar honoring Posidaeja. The Minoans used triton shells as ritual trumpets and rhytons. So you could use your shell to pour out liquid offerings to Posidaeja. Or you could simply set it on the altar. If you have a triton shell that has been drilled to make it into a trumpet, you can blow it in her honor (three blasts at a time).

As the Mother of the Waters, Posidaeja's favorite offering is, you guessed it, water. You'll want to use water from a natural source. If you don't have a lake, stream, or river handy (or the ocean!), you can use bottled spring water. Please don't use treated tap water, but water from a well is acceptable. Posidaeja also loves flowers and seashells as offerings. On the beach, you can make her an artistic design out of seashells on the sand and then let the tide take them back out to her. You can set fresh flowers on the altar as a gift to her. But if you want to make a really special offering, make a garland or wreath of flowers (with biodegradable materials only, please) and toss it into a body of water to give it to her.

Divination with Posidaeja can involve several different methods. A collection of seashells that you toss onto a cloth (or the sand at the beach) will offer patterns and images that you can read. You can scry in any kind of moving water: ocean waves, the flow of a river or stream, even a fountain in a city plaza. Posidaeja also seems to like pendulums, especially those with clear, white, pearlescent, or blue-toned stones as the weight. She typically provides insight into the emotional and relationship aspects of a situation more than any nuts-and-bolts practical aspects.

If you're embodying Posidaeja in a ritual, you'll want to dress in a way that makes people think of water, especially the sea. Shades of blue and blue-green in fabrics that drape and flow are good choices. You could try jagged hems that suggest seaweed swaying in the current as you move. Soft, gentle bits of shiny material (sequins, glitter, lamé fabric) evoke the glint of light on water. Pearls are a good choice as well, preferably real ones; freshwater pearls aren't nearly as expensive as saltwater ones.

Ariadne

Pronunciation: air-ee-ADD-nee or ahr-ee-AHD-nay
Epithets: *Lady of the Labyrinth, Queen Bee, Queen of the Dead, Lily of the Fields*

Here's a goddess who ended up being demoted to a maiden, a mere mortal, in later Greek mythology. It took a lot of people digging into the ancient sources for a long time to figure out that she was so much more than just a girl with a ball of string.

In the well-known Greek myth, Ariadne's main function is to help Theseus find his way out of the Labyrinth after he has killed the Minotaur and rescued his fellow Athenian youths from the horrors of the depraved Minoan court. But Theseus didn't exist in Minoan times. He's a Greek culture hero, invented centuries after the collapse of Minoan civilization, to 'advertise' the Greeks as modern and advanced compared to the 'primitive' Minoans. So if Theseus wasn't around in ancient Crete, what did Ariadne do with her time there? A lot more than just play with string.

Her most famous attribute is the labyrinth, which turns out to be not a confusing maze at all, but a spiraling pattern that has only one route: one way in and the same way back out. You can't get lost. This type of design is called a unicursal (one route) maze. Labyrinths have been found all over the world dating back to very ancient times, so this is a concept that goes back to the early days of humanity. The term labyrinth is related to the word labrys, the double axe that's such a famous emblem of Minoan civilization. Though the etymology isn't clear, most people take labyrinth to mean 'House of the Double Axe.' This means the labrys is also Ariadne's symbol.

The labyrinth is a shamanic tool that helps the spiritual practitioner go deep within their own subconscious as well as journey to the Underworld. The Crane Dance, which goes along with the labyrinth in mythology, probably began in early Minoan times when the people danced on the circular threshing floors at the end of the harvest. These early dances would have been performed in honor of the Ancestors, and Ariadne is their queen. Homer's tales go back to Mycenaean times, when bits and pieces of Minoan culture might still have been around. He said the labyrinth was Ariadne's ceremonial dancing ground. In the harvest-time versions of these dances in MMP, Ariadne is aided by the Melissae, the ancestral bee-goddesses who have their own entry later in this section.

Together with her brother Tauros Asterion in his form as the Minotaur, Ariadne guides us through the labyrinth into the cave of our own darkness, our own shadow self. There we can confront our inner demons and learn how to become whole again. Our modern society can make it difficult to accept the parts of ourselves that aren't "goodness and light." But Ariadne understands that we are multi-faceted beings. It's the light that makes the shadow, and we must learn to appreciate and accept both.

Because Ariadne has access to the Underworld, we view her as a psychopomp, a conductor of the souls of the dead on their journey to the afterlife. She helps the living as a guide for those who wish to meet the Ancestors, honor them, and ask their blessing on our lives. She's a helper and healer as well, leading us into our own depths so that we can mend our wounds and restore ourselves to wholeness.

Ariadne also has a role to play in the precursor to one of the more famous bits of later Greek religion, the Eleusinian Mysteries. This ten-day-long sacred festival, based on the tale of Demeter and Persephone, developed from a much earlier agrarian cult that goes back to Minoan times. The Hellenic Greek version of the myth portrays Persephone as a victim, abducted by Hades and imprisoned in the Underworld until her mother, Demeter, can talk Zeus into demanding her release. This storyline reinforces the Hellenic Greek cultural values of submissive women who are effectively the property of the men in their lives and who cannot speak for themselves. It's interesting to note that Demeter and

Persephone are probably pre-Greek goddesses who were already being worshiped on the Greek mainland when the Indo-Europeans arrived. So it's likely that their original story was closer to the one we use in MMP than the one the Greeks developed.

The Minoans had a society in which goddesses—and women—acted under their own power. The Minoan version of the Mysteries involved not Demeter and Persephone, but Rhea and Ariadne. Since Ariadne is associated with the Underworld and the Ancestors, we think she went there willingly in the original version of the myth and simply returned to the World Above when Rhea let her know it was time to bring the rain at the beginning of the new agricultural cycle. Ariadne comes with the first green sprouts in the fields after planting time, which is in the autumn in the Mediterranean. In a sense, Ariadne is the grain itself, in a way very similar to northern European grain gods like John Barleycorn. A fuller version of the story of the Mysteries is included in Chapter 4.

This mythological cycle, with Ariadne descending to the Underworld then returning again each year, symbolizes the concept of rebirth. This includes not just the renewal of plant life each year, but also the idea of the eternal soul that is reborn again and again in reincarnation. The idea of rebirth may have something to do with the name of the Eleusinian Mysteries. The city where the festival was held in classical Greece is called Eleusis, which is a pre-Greek name probably related to the name of the goddess Eileithyia. We know that one of the secrets that were taught in the Eleusinian Mysteries is the idea of the soul being eternal. In the ancient world, this would have included the idea of the soul residing in the Underworld or among the Ancestors between physical incarnations.

There's another aspect of the story of Demeter and Persephone that we should consider. When Persephone was in the Underworld (remember, she was abducted there by Hades), she ate several pomegranate seeds. According to the Hellenic Greek version of the tale, eating those seeds was the act that doomed Persephone to keep returning to the Underworld each year. But what if the original version didn't work that way? What if Ariadne was the Underworld goddess and pomegranates were sacred to her as the food of the dead? Then she would eat pomegranate seeds to honor those in her care, and she would do it willingly, with love. She would also willingly return to the Underworld every year in the appropriate season to take care of the souls there. We should consider the possibility that caring for the dead was once an honored, and honorable, task and not something that would have been done only under duress.

In connection with the Mysteries, the poppy is sacred to Ariadne. In MMP, we consider it a gift from her mother Rhea, in whose grain fields poppies have long been grown alongside the wheat and barley. The Minoans produced opium from the poppies they grew. It was probably used for both medicinal and hallucinogenic purposes. So the poppy is a sacred flower that helps the living connect with the dead in ritual, just as Ariadne connects the worlds of the living and the dead in her yearly cycle. Opium was also a way to ease a person's transition, allowing a death without pain, and possibly a magical substance that could provide healing to the souls of the dead in the Underworld.

Throughout the ancient world, red foods like pomegranates were considered the food of the dead because they were the color of blood. In later cultures such as the Greeks, the idea was that the dead were jealous of the living and wanted to drink their blood in order to come back to life. So people offered red food to the dead to placate them and keep them from bothering or endangering the living. But I suspect that earlier cultures, particularly the Minoans, had a different view. The realm of the Ancestors was where souls resided after death but also before birth—newborn babies received their souls from the Ancestors. The color red, then, wouldn't stand for the jealousy of the dead. Instead, it would symbolize the blood that binds the generations of both living and dead, the blood that we now know contains the DNA of all our ancestors going back to the very beginning of time. It might also symbolize the blood of birth, when each person's soul emerges from the Underworld to join us anew.

Returning to the subject of the Eleusinian Mysteries and their original Minoan version, in MMP the labyrinth works as a symbol of Ariadne's descent into the Underworld (that's the path to the center of the labyrinth) and her ascent back up into our world (that's the path from the center back out to the outside of the labyrinth). So it can be our gateway to a rebirth of whatever sort we choose to focus on: the seasons, life changes, healing, and so on. This can take a number of different forms: walking a full-size labyrinth, meditating on an image of a labyrinth, or 'walking' a finger labyrinth (tracing the path with your finger).

While she's in the Underworld caring for the spirits of the dead, Ariadne is the Queen Bee: the head of the Melissae, the bee-spirit goddesses who are the guardians of the spirits of the dead. The bee is an ancient symbol for the soul, and a buzzing sound like a hive of bees is a common experience of people who are entering shamanic trance to travel to the Underworld. In her connection with the Melissae, Ariadne becomes almost a spirit of the dead herself, a kind of sacred ancestor who tends the souls of her people.

Another symbol we associate with Ariadne is red Asiatic lilies. The red color may be a reminder of the Underworld and the Ancestors, but it may also symbolize menstrual or birthing blood. Lilies were very popular in Minoan art and are found in frescoes, jewelry, and pottery. In addition to red, sometimes lilies were painted white on a red background, a reversal that underscores the importance of light and dark in Minoan art and religion: both are a part of the world and of our inner selves.

If you'd like to include Ariadne in your sacred space, you might choose a figurine to represent her. Many people like to use reproductions of the Snake Goddess figurine, though the Snake Goddess could also represent Ariadne's mother Rhea, the Grain-Mother (snakes eat the rodents that eat the grain). There are also goddess figurines that hold labryses; these are appropriate since the labrys is Ariadne's symbol. Of course, you don't need a figurine at all. You could represent Ariadne with the labrys or the labyrinth. A finger labyrinth or a piece of artwork that includes a labyrinth would be a lovely addition to your altar. A labrys in the color of your choosing, and perhaps a pomegranate or a piece of artwork depicting pomegranates, would go well, too. Lilies—the actual flowers or images of them—would be a lovely addition to your sacred space. Many people find that shades of pink and lavender evoke Ariadne's energy for them, so you could choose altar cloths, candles, and other items in those colors.

Ariadne happily accepts wine as an offering: red wine for her Underworld aspect and white wine for her face as the goddess of green growing things. Since she rises into the World Above with the first sprouts of grain in the fields (or *as* those sprouts, depending on how you look at it) you can also offer her sprouted grains. Wheat berries, whole rye grains, and barley can all be soaked and sprouted and then offered to her. Wheat grass (whole, not made into a smoothie) also works as an offering to her World Above aspect. To honor her Underworld aspect, you can offer pomegranates—the whole fruit, the seeds, or the juice—as well as poppyseeds.

Divination with Ariadne as your guide might involve ears of grain (wheat or barley) or pomegranate seeds tossed onto a surface to discover the patterns and images they contain. The Labyrinth is also a sort of divination tool, in that it helps you find answers to life's questions. Though Ariadne is a loving helper and guide, she tends to like people to find their own answers rather than having her hand them over on a platter, so expect to have to work a little if you do divination with her.

If you're going to embody Ariadne in a ritual, you'll want to think about which aspect of her you're focusing on. Do you want people to see the goddess of the green sprouts who rises from the Underworld to bring the rains that soften the soil and ready it for planting? Or do you want people to see the guardian and comforter of the spirits of the dead, the head of the Melissae and the queen of the Underworld? Shades of pink and lavender work well for either of these, but the Underworld version should be more subdued, more ghostly, if you will, perhaps with just a touch of gold to point to Ariadne's connection with the Melissae.

Arachne

Pronunciation: ah-RACK-nee
*Epithets: Lady Fate, Thread-Spinner, Web-Weaver, Ananke (ah-
NAHN-kay, "necessity")*

This ancient fate goddess found herself demoted first to a human
woman and then to a spider in Greek myth, though her divinity
shows through in the perfect weaving that gets her in trouble in
that tale. She's a weaver of a sort, of course, but Arachne is, above
all, the spinner of the thread of fate—the thread that her sister
Ariadne winds through the Labyrinth to help us find our way.

The name Arachne comes from the pre-Greek (Pelasgian)
word for spider; we don't know what the Minoans called their
fate goddess. It's likely that "spider" was one of her epithets, since
spiders spin threads and webs, longtime symbols of the winding
and tangled paths of human lives. In MMP we also call this
goddess Ananke, a name that means *necessity* and that can also be
interpreted to mean the laws of nature. Though the Orphics, many
centuries after the fall of Minoan civilization, considered Ananke
to be a cosmic creator-goddess like our Ourania, in MMP she's the
goddess of fate.

Each person's fate, the thread of their life, runs from birth to
death, so Arachne is connected with the goddess Eileithyia, who
midwifes the beginning and end of each person's lifetime. In
addition to being the midwife-goddess, Eileithyia is also the
Underworld face of our Sun goddess Therasia. Arachne is
connected with Therasia, of course, because the fate goddess is
Therasia's daughter. Throughout Eurasia, Sun goddesses have
long been associated with fate, since it's in days that we number
our lives, from one sunrise to the next. So not only does Arachne
weave the webs of fate, she's also pretty tangled up in the web of
relationships among the Minoan gods and goddesses. She
probably doesn't mind.

We don't know how the ancient Minoans understood the idea
of fate, or whether they felt as powerless against the whims of the
gods as the later Greeks apparently did. Our experience with
Arachne in the modern world suggests that she's not so much the

designer of each person's individual destiny as she is the one who tallies our decisions, for good or ill, and keeps track of where we're going. In other words, she's the Counter of Consequences, and it's her thread, her web that we either climb to great heights or hang ourselves with.

Like the Arachne of Greek myth, the goddess in the MMP pantheon is associated with spinning, weaving, and the other textile arts. Natural fibers like wool and flax are hers, as are yarn, thread, and finished fabric. Dyeing cloth is a related activity whose patron goddess we call Potnia Chromaton, Lady of the Colors. She is closely tied to both Therasia and Arachne.

The thread that Ariadne sets loose in the Labyrinth is often described as being colored red, so red thread in particular is a symbol of Arachne in MMP. In this case, the color red may stand for life's blood or for the vitality of a person's life. It's also possible the red indicates that the thread was dyed with murex dye, sacred to Arachne's mother Therasia. The Labyrinth thread is also sometimes described as gold, Therasia's other sacred color. Note that I haven't been able to find any reference to the actual color of the thread in any ancient writer's work, so the color choices may be modern interpolations of the mythos. Still, they work for us since they correspond with the colors we're already using for these deities.

Of course, the spider is also one of Arachne's symbols: not a vicious bug (though we don't recommend playing with venomous ones) but a beautiful creature that spins threads that are both delicate and strong. Spiders have been connected with spinning for ages, probably since the first people figured out how to twist cordage out of plant fibers. As our spinning and weaving skills developed, the spider continued its association with these human activities.

If you'd like to dedicate an altar to Arachne, you can start with either spider imagery or the idea of spinning thread (or both—it's not an either/or world, after all). As a fate goddess, she isn't terribly colorful: black, white, and grey should form the basis of your altar's color scheme. But the red or gold thread she spins can be a focal point, perhaps in the form of a ball of yarn. In Chapter 7, you can find instructions for making a simple drop spindle. You can set the spindle by itself on your altar, or you can spin thread with it (natural fibers only, please) and include that on your altar as well. The time and effort of learning to spin can be an offering to Arachne.

Figurines that can represent Arachne on your altar might be a little hard to come by. If you can find a figurine (or other art, like a painting or photo) of a woman spinning, that would be a good choice. Sometimes, figurines of the Norse goddess Frigga show her spinning. You could use one of these figurines as long as they aren't already dedicated to Frigga and as long as you remove any evidence of her name, runes, or other non-Minoan marks on the statue. A plain female figurine, without any symbols and who isn't holding any objects, can also be dedicated to her. A spider figurine can also stand for Arachne on an altar. If you're going to develop a relationship with Arachne, it's a good idea to learn to like spiders. I promise you, if you don't seek them out, they'll find you.

Fiber arts activities (spinning, weaving, knitting, crocheting, sewing) can be dedicated to Arachne as offerings, as can the finished products of these activities. Making useful items using any of these skills and then donating them to those in need (shelters, hospitals, and so on) is a powerful offering to Arachne in her guise as Ananke (necessity). She also accepts offerings of red wine, the darker, the better. She seems to like the dark of night better than the daylight, so time your work with her accordingly.

Arachne is especially fond of pendulums for divination, preferably with a weight that's made of a black or dark grey stone. I've also found that she can aid divination that's done by the tossing of seeds (dried grain kernels, poppyseed, or sesame seed) onto a cloth. Interestingly, plaid and checkered cloths seem to give the best results, even better than those with a spiderweb design on them. If you focus well and listen intently, Arachne will usually offer you help. But be aware that she doesn't sugar-coat anything.

Don't ask a question if you don't want to hear the hard, cold answer.

If you're embodying Arachne in a ritual, you'll want to stick with the black/grey/white color scheme. Silver, rather than gold, is the best choice for jewelry or other ornamentation, and hematite works well, too. Like most of the Minoan deities, she prefers natural fibers to synthetic ones. You can cover your face if you like to emphasize the idea that our fate is unknown to us, but it's not required like it is for clergy who are embodying Ourania. Clergy who are embodying Arachne in ritual may carry the red or gold thread, though if Ariadne is also being honored in the rite, at some point Arachne should hand it off it to her.

Antheia

Pronunciation: an-THEE-ah, an-THAY-ah

Epithets: *Star of the Sea, Fair Blossom, Morning Star, Evening Star*

Antheia is the Minoan face of the goddess Aphrodite. She's our goddess of love and beauty. How did we come to call her Antheia? It's a name the Greeks used for one of the Kharites (the Graces, who were Aphrodite's attendants). But the Greek writer Hesychius tells us that Antheia was the name used for Aphrodite at Knossos. Presumably this was a bit of mythos that survived the centuries, since Knossos was destroyed about 1350 BCE, two millennia before Hesychius wrote his works.

Aphrodite appears to be a pre-Greek goddess whose worship originated on the island of Cyprus. From there, she traveled westward to Crete and elsewhere around the eastern Mediterranean. One very simple method for figuring out whether we're on the right track with Minoan spirituality is to ask the deities themselves. When we tried the name Antheia, the goddess we were expecting (the Minoan face of Aphrodite) responded positively.

Though Greek mythology portrays Aphrodite as petty, vain, and vindictive, we don't find Antheia to be any of those things. She is beautiful, yes, but it's a loveliness that she shares freely with the world, not one born of competition or jealousy. She helps us find beauty in the world: in ourselves, in each other, in nature, even in the tasks of our daily lives. And she helps us realize the power of beauty to connect us with the divine. A pretty flower, a twinkling star, a warm smile—these are things that remind us that the whole world is sacred, that the divine isn't "out there somewhere" but right here, within each and every one of us.

In the MMP pantheon, Antheia is Posidaeja's daughter, so we can think of her as being born from the sea-foam, though without the need for any severed genitals being tossed into the mix as happens in Aphrodite's Greek creation story. Because Antheia is associated with the sea, or more specifically, with the seashore, we consider water birds to be hers: geese, ducks, swans. Flowers spring up under Antheia's feet as she walks along the sea-coast. These flowers might be sea daffodils (*Pancratium maritimum*), a white, lily-like wildflower native to Crete that has been revered since ancient times. Also known as the sand lily or lily of Knossos, the sea daffodil grows along the dunes and beaches of Crete and is currently endangered.

In addition to the sea daffodil, we associate yellow and gold flowers, as well as the color golden yellow, with Antheia. In fact, wreaths and necklaces of fresh flowers in any color are also her thing, though yellow and white flowers are her preference. The crown daisy (*Glebionis coronaria*) is native to the Mediterranean. It's a lovely yellow-and-white flower, but any kind of daisy or other yellow-and-white flower would be a good choice, as would flowers that are all white or all yellow.

Like the Greek Aphrodite, Antheia is associated with the planet Venus. From this association, we have the symbol of the eight-petaled rosette as an icon for her. But unlike Aphrodite, who had quite a fling with the war god Ares, and unlike the Venus-planet goddesses from the Near East like Inanna, Ishtar, and Astarte, Antheia isn't associated with war. The Minoans weren't a warlike people. They had no interest in conquering other cultures, only selling goods to them. We suspect the Minoans may have asked Antheia's aid in avoiding war, but that's the only war connection we've found with her so far (unless you consider the competition of the marketplace to be a kind of battlefield, in which case Antheia could be called on to highlight the beauty of the goods you're offering for sale).

In MMP we also connect Antheia with Ourania, our Great Cosmic Mother. One of Aphrodite's titles was Ourania, in other words, Queen of Heaven. In MMP we don't view Antheia as a cosmic or heavenly goddess, but we do associate her with the starry sky. The ancients considered Venus, along with the other planets, to be special kinds of stars, since they moved against the background of the other stars in the night sky. A starry sky with Venus glowing brightly near the horizon, reflecting in the surface of the sea, is an image we connect with Antheia—and one that can be used to call to her.

The common myrtle (*Myrtus communis*), a flowering shrub that's native to the Mediterranean, is also one of Antheia's symbols. The tiny, five-petaled flowers are a delicate white, later yielding blue-black berries. Myrtle berries and leaves have been used since ancient times to flavor food and drink and to relieve fever and pain. And the little starry flowers are said to look like the twinkling planet Venus in the night sky. Myrtle doesn't grow in my area, but chickweed (*Stellaria media*) does. It, too, has tiny, five-petaled white flowers, and I've found that Antheia will happily accept fresh chickweed on her altar, especially if it's in bloom.

If you'd like to set up an altar to Antheia, you can start with her colors: yellow, gold, and white. Use this color scheme for your altar cloth and other items like candleholders. Figurines of Aphrodite will work for Antheia, as long as they don't have Aphrodite's name painted or embossed on them anywhere. Her altar should include things you find beautiful. Clear, white, and golden stones are good choices, as are star-shaped objects and eight-petaled rosettes. Since her mother is Posidaeja, you can include seashells, too. And of course, water birds are hers, so images or figurines of ducks, geese, and swans are a good choice; you could include feathers if you like, for instance if you happen to find a fallen feather from the geese and ducks at your local pond.

In terms of offerings, Antheia enjoys fresh flowers, especially in shades of yellow and white. You can lay loose flowers on your altar or set up a bouquet in a vase. If you're going to have an active relationship with Antheia, it's a good idea to dedicate a vase to her and keep a fresh floral arrangement on your altar all the time. You could also drape the altar with wreaths or garlands of flowers. And yes, you can make daisy chains and dandelion necklaces to honor her. In terms of libations, she especially likes myrtle liqueur (Mirto), though white and rosé wine are also good choices. If you happen to have a myrtle plant in your herb garden, you can offer the fresh berries and leafy stems. For offerings of incense, choose sweet floral fragrances over spicy or musky ones.

One of the most amazing types of divination I've experienced with Antheia as my guide is seeking patterns in the drops of dew that I find on outdoor plants and flowers first thing in the morning. She's also quite fond of water that's spraying from fountains, sprinklers, and similar devices and can help you scry in those. I think that's her connection with her mother Posidaeja showing through there. You can look in spraying water for patterns and images, especially in the reflections of light among the droplets. If you want to try a more traditional form of divination with Antheia, go to a body of water that has a flock of ducks or geese. They can be hanging out on the shore or paddling in the water. Wait until they take off, then look for patterns in their movements. Don't pluck the petals off of flowers ("She loves me, she loves me not...") unless you want to offend her.

If you'll be embodying Antheia in ritual, think of beauty and love as you choose your garments and accessories. Shades of golden yellow and white are the best choices for clothing, in soft, natural fabrics that drape well. Go for bright gold jewelry instead of silver or antique gold tones. Antheia is about beauty, love, and consensual pleasure, not raciness or lewdness, so bear that in mind as you decide how to dress. Feel free to use as much makeup as you're comfortable with, style your hair in a fancy "do," and dab on some sweet perfume. Then let your beauty—and hers—shine through.

Tauros Asterion

Pronunciation: TOH-rohs ah-STAY-ree-on
Epithets: Great Bull, Cretan Bull, Starry One, Bull of Heaven
Tauros Asterion is much more than just an animal god. His name means 'bull' (Tauros) and 'starry one' (Asterion). If that makes you think of the constellation Taurus, that's a good start. There was already a bovine (bull and cow) cult in western Anatolia when the Minoans' ancestors migrated from there to Crete in the Neolithic era. And the association of the constellation Taurus with a bull probably goes back as far as the Paleolithic, if the artwork in the Lascaux cave is any indication. So it's likely that Tauros' worship is pretty old. But in MMP we focus on him as part of the Minoan pantheon from the Bronze Age.

We get his second name, Asterion, from three references in classical literature. The first two are from Pseudo-Apollodorus and Diodorus Siculus (say that three times fast!). Pseudo-Apollodorus was the pen name of a Greek or Roman author who lived in the first or second century BCE, and Diodorus Siculus was a Greek historian who lived in the first century BCE. So these men were writing about 1400 years after the destruction of the Minoan cities, collecting up fragments of Minoan myth that had managed to make it through the centuries via a combination of oral and written sources. Here's what they have to say about Asterion: "A son of Teutamus, and king of the Cretans, who married Europa after she had been carried to Crete by Zeus. He also brought up the three sons, Minos, Sarpedon, and Rhadamanthys, whom she had by the father of the gods." (Apollod. iii. 1. § 2, &c.; Diod. iv. 60.) So he's pretty heavily entangled in Minoan mythos in a very garbled kind of way. Teutamus was a 4th century BCE Macedonian military commander, so he must have been added to the story at a very late date. But Europa is our Minoan cow-goddess (see her entry below for more details) who was hijacked into the Greek mythology by the sadly common device of being abducted by Zeus. And Minos, Sarpedon, and Rhadamanthys are a triplicity of Minoan Underworld gods who are discussed at length under the entry for Minos further down in this chapter. So we have a good handful of Minoan deities linked with Asterion, who in this case is called a king, in spite of the fact that there's no evidence the Minoans ever had a monarchy.

The other reference to Asterion in classical literature comes from Pausanias, a Greek traveler and geographer who lived in the second century CE. Here's what he wrote about Asterion: "In the market-place of Troizenos [in Argolis] is a temple of Artemis Soteira [Savior] with images of the goddess. It was said that the temple was founded and the name Soteria [Savior] given by Theseus when he returned from Crete after overcoming Asterion the son of Minos." (Pausanias, Description of Greece 2.31.1) So here, Asterion is Minos' son, while the other two writers called him Minos' stepfather. This shows just how garbled and confused myths can become as they're passed down over time, especially during chaotic eras like the Bronze Age collapse. Asterion's mention in Pausanias' work is the tidbit that Karl Kerenyi used to link him with the Minotaur. In MMP we do consider the Minotaur to be one of Tauros Asterion's faces, but that's not all there is to this multi-faceted god.

As Rhea's son, Tauros is a very earthy god. Think of the sound of aurochs' hooves thundering across the ground, shaking the Earth beneath your feet. Think of cattle grazing, their teeth cropping the fresh, green grass as their droppings fertilize the soil. But remember also the cool, sweet darkness of the cave, the brown soil, the smooth stones—the caves in the hills of western Anatolia where the Minoans' ancestors lived, and the caves in the sacred mountains of Crete where the Minoans' beliefs and skills blossomed into a marvelous culture that lasted for centuries.

This earthiness means that Tauros understands physical existence better than some other deities do. While we might call on him as the Minotaur (along with his sister Ariadne) for psychological and emotional healing, we can look to Tauros Asterion to help us with physical ailments. He and his mother

Rhea together make a powerful pair for correcting many of the things that can go wrong with the human body. Of course, you should always seek appropriate professional medical care. But it never hurts to have a few more members on your healing team.

So that's Tauros' earthy side. But like Antheia, who also has a connection with Ourania in addition to her "planetary" mother Posidaeja, Tauros Asterion links with both Rhea and Ourania. He has an aspect that goes beyond the Earth, to the stars. Taurus is one of the oldest constellations. It has been linked with the form of a bull for millennia, possibly tens of thousands of years. In the Lascaux cave, which dates to about 17,000 years ago, there's a beautiful painting of a bull with the Pleiades and the Hyades dotted in just the right places for the picture to represent the constellation Taurus. This connection with Ourania gives Tauros a broad outlook, what you might call a cosmic point of view.

In many cultures, spots on the hides of animals are symbolic representations of the stars in the night sky. Minoan art includes many images of spotted bulls, and in MMP we take these to represent the starry or cosmic aspect of Tauros Asterion. The bull in the famous Bull Leapers fresco from Knossos is an obvious example. But there are also ceramic rhytons (libation pitchers) in the shape of spotted bulls as well as chariots and ikria (ship compartments) that are depicted as being covered in spotted cowhide.

Two of Tauros Asterion's faces are the Minotaur and Zagreus. You can read about them in detail in their separate listings below. To develop a relationship with those aspects of this god, you'll want to use those specific names (Minotaur and Zagreus). To connect with him on a broader level, call him Tauros Asterion.

If you'd like to set up an altar to Tauros Asterion, you can start with an earthy color scheme in shades of brown and tan. You can also add in some green tones if you like, a reminder that Rhea is his earthly mother. The sacred horns are, of course, one of his symbols. Bull figurines work well here, as do leather and cowhide (with hair still attached) objects like boxes and journals. An actual bovine horn would be a powerful addition to Tauros' altar. To direct a little energy toward his Asterion aspect, an image of the constellation Taurus is a good choice. You could simply paint white dots on a piece of black paper or posterboard or print out a constellation image (NASA is a great source of public domain astronomy images). A photo of the Taurus bull painting from the Lascaux cave would be a great choice, too. Bear in mind that what you're aiming for isn't so much animalistic as earthy. While Tauros Asterion isn't exactly an urbanite, he has a certain "cultured-ness" that often overpowers any primitive or rustic energy.

In terms of offerings, he appreciates dark red wine and port. And yes, you can go for the kind of red wine that's called bull's blood (Bika Vére, Sangre de Toro, and others). He's also fond of having physical labor dedicated to him as an offering, especially anything earthy like digging ditches or cleaning the litter out of a local park. If you're likely to sweat while you're doing he, he'll probably enjoy it as an offering.

If you'd like to do divination with Tauros, you'll need to collect up some stones, preferably natural and unpolished, and a piece of leather large enough to use as a casting cloth. A piece of black natural-fiber fabric will also work, either plain or painted with white dots to mark the constellations. Use your favorite method to attain a meditative state, then toss the stones onto the cloth and look to see what patterns they form (and listen to what Tauros has to say).

If you're embodying him in ritual, you'll want to spend some time beforehand getting used to his energy, even if you've done this kind of work with other deities in the past. Tauros' energy is heavy and large and has a shamanic-style animal component that takes some getting used to. In terms of your appearance, you don't need to wear a bull mask. In fact, a mask is a better choice for the Minotaur than for Tauros Asterion. But you should go for an earthy theme, with clothing in shades of brown and tan, preferably leather. It doesn't have to look terribly primitive or "stone age," but it shouldn't be obviously modern (in other words, a biker jacket with a dozen shiny silver zippers all over it isn't the kind of leather to go for here).

Korydallos

Pronunciation: koh-ree-dah-LOS
Epithets: Red Champion, Red Warrior, the Lark

This enigmatic god comes to us via the fascinating field of dance ethnography. The Red Champion still exists in folk dances around the Mediterranean today. A shamanic spirit warrior of a sort, he's the son of an ancient goddess figure. He may very well predate the Minoans, possibly going back as far as the beginning of farming in the Neolithic, given the content of the dances he appears in. But our experience with him in MMP links him with Therasia, so that's how he fits into our pantheon: he's her son.

He's one of the three Young Gods, each one a son of one of our mother goddesses. In that role, he acts as an intermediary between the people and the Mothers. Like his brothers, he's forever young: youthful, energetic, exuberant. But of course, he's also old, as old as the gods themselves. So he's wise but also playful, which can be a nice change sometimes.

One popular item in ancient Crete was the dagger, an object made via metalsmithing, the purview of Korydallos' mother Therasia. Young men owned daggers as elaborate as they could afford. They all had bronze blades, and the fanciest ones had gold hilts. They wore these daggers upright (with the handle up and the blade downward) at the waist right next to their codpieces. You can't get a more obvious phallic symbol than that.

For a long time we thought these daggers might have been associated with Dionysus because of the sexual symbolism—the Greeks certainly portrayed Dionysus as promiscuous. But in MMP we've come to relate the dagger more to Korydallos instead. After all, metalsmithing is the craft Therasia gives her blessing to. And some of the dances we find Korydallos in involve bladed weapons. I find it interesting that traditional Cretan dress for men well into the 20th century, and still occasionally today, includes an upright dagger worn at the waist in very much the same style as the ancient Minoans.

But if you're looking for Korydallos' spirit weapon in the form of a dagger or sword, you're not going to find it. Instead, he carries a staff. Like his brothers, he's a shamanic god, traveling between the worlds, and his staff acts like a World Tree as he moves energy around. He's not a psychopomp the way Dionysus is, and he isn't nearly as earthy as Tauros. Instead, you might think of him as a dancer, not just in those folk dances, but in the dance of life itself.

Korydallos' connection with smithcraft leads us to the idea that Daedalus is one of his faces, just as the Minotaur is one of Tauros Asterion's faces. You can find more details about Daedalus' connection to Korydallos in his listing later in this chapter. Daedalus is a cunning and clever deity, and in MMP, he's the god of smithcraft and inventing.

Korydallos is a joyous god. He sparkles and shines, and he has a sense of humor—sometimes a fairly trickstery one. Like his namesake the lark, he flies merrily above the shadows of life, singing a jubilant song and reminding us not to take ourselves too seriously. He loves wordplay and riddles, so be aware that if you're listening for messages from him, he may make you work for the answers you seek. Those of us who have relationships with him hear him laughing on a regular basis, as if he is overcome by the sheer joy of existence. Hang out with him long enough, and that joy will rub off on you, too.

In MMP we connect Korydallos with bronze and with the color red. He's especially fond of red ochre, a natural iron-rich pigment that's been used in a sacred context since the Paleolithic. Sometimes he appears to people as golden all over or with thick golden hair almost like a lion's mane (and very different from the dark brown to black hair the Minoans had). Something many people don't realize is that new bronze, if it's well-polished, looks very much like gold and not like the dark, brownish metal we're used to thinking of when we see the aged, corroded bronze artifacts the archaeologists have dug up.

If you want to set up an altar to Korydallos, begin with his colors: red and gold (the gold color of bright new bronze) as well as the darker bronze tones. He's perfectly happy with metal objects on the altar, but preferably not iron or steel. He likes bronze and brass a lot. Brass candleholders, plates, and bowls are good choices for his altar. In keeping with the idea of brightness, set up his altar in a well-lit area instead of a dark corner. Near a window where the sunlight shines in is a good choice. He likes candles in shades of red and yellow/gold and is quite fond of the kind of deep yellow beeswax that smells like honey. He also likes oil lamps, especially if you use a fruity olive oil as the fuel.

If you want to make an offering to Korydallos, think of joyful things: flowers, sweet-smelling incense, honey, sweet wine or mead. He's quite fond of homemade bread, still warm from the oven, but then, who isn't? He also appreciates acts of kindness, particularly those toward our fellow human beings. So if you want to do some volunteer work and dedicate it to him as an offering, consider helping out at a nursing home, a homeless shelter, or a center for disadvantaged youth.

Divination with Korydallos can be a bit frustrating, since his tendency to play games can generate layers of riddles and hidden meanings no matter what divination method you're using. But if you want to give it a try, one method that works well with him is to fill a light-colored bowl with a golden liquid (mead, white wine, lemonade) or fill a yellow bowl with clear water. Either way, what you're going for is a shimmering golden circle in front of you. Get yourself into a relaxed, meditative state using your preferred method. Hold a small white stone very close to the surface of the liquid, right over the center of the bowl, then drop it in. Its motion will create ripples in the liquid. Watch those ripples, allowing your vision to soften, and see what you can see. Allow for the possibility that you'll have to dig down through layers of symbolism in what you see, or you might need to sleep on it and let your subconscious figure out the meaning for you.

If you're going to embody Korydallos in ritual, the important thing to remember is that you want to project a sense of joy.

Choose clothing in shades of red, yellow, and gold. Depending on the nature of your ritual, if it's a joyful one that's not too serious, you could even go for gold lamé—yes, Korydallos has that kind of sense of humor! But generally speaking, you want to give the impression of the kind of honest happiness that children have. Your clothing can look either modern or timeless, depending on your personal preference. Any jewelry should be gold tone or polished bronze. Golden metal bells are also appropriate for Korydallos—ankle bells or a bell as a pendant, for instance. Remember to smile and laugh!

Dionysus
Pronunciation: dye-oh-NYE-sus
Epithets: The Undiluted One, the Liberator, Iacchus
Most people have heard of Dionysus. The general public tends to think of him as the 'party god'—the one with the wine and the drugs and the orgies. But there's far more to Dionysus than just having a good time. He's a psychopomp and the bringer of sacred ecstasy, a god whose origins probably go as far back as the beginnings of wine-making. The Greeks combined the Minoan god with a Phrygian ecstatic god to get the multi-faceted Dionysus we know from classical mythology. But before the classical age, before the Bronze Age collapse, Dionysus was being worshiped on Crete and in parts of Greece.

His name is known from several Linear B inscriptions, written with characters that spell out *di-wo-nu-so*. Though some scholars have attempted to link the 'dio' part of his name to the Indo-European word root for god (dio/deo/theo), the Linear B version tells us that his name was originally pronounced 'diwo' or 'divo' and isn't from that word root after all. Language is a funny thing, and words change over time as speakers unconsciously decide what's easier to pronounce and what's not. The w/v sound (written in early Greek with a character called a digamma) disappeared from the Greek language somewhere between Mycenaean and classical Greek, so it was simply dropped from Dionysus' name. If you want to call him by a name that's closer to the one the Minoans used, you could try Divonusos (dee-VOH-new-sos).

First and foremost, Dionysus is associated with wine and the grapes the wine is made from. In MMP, we commemorate his death every year at the grape harvest in early autumn; see the Feast of Grapes in Chapter 4 for more details. The ancient Minoans had some sort of sacred celebration at the grape harvest, though we don't know for certain what it might have looked like. You can think of the grape harvest festival as similar to the grain-god harvest celebrations in the more northern parts of early Europe: the god dies to give us something that nourishes us and makes our lives better. Like most death-harvest celebrations, it probably would have included both solemn parts and a certain amount of revelry. (Just in case you were missed it in the entry earlier in this chapter, the grain-deity in MMP is Ariadne: she is the grain itself, coming up from the Underworld with the first green sprouts in the fields and dying with the harvest. But we're talking about Dionysus here, so let's get back to him.)

Part of Dionysus' gift to the people is his ability to take us out of our ordinary mindset and allow us to forget the weight and the woes of everyday life, if only just for a while. Purposeful drunkenness during Dionysian rituals was considered a sign of blessing or even possession by the god in the ancient world. I suspect that inebriation outside of these special times was not looked on quite so kindly.

Dionysus isn't just the god of wine. He's the god of the grape harvest in general. In addition to wine, the Minoans drank fresh grape juice, ate the fresh fruit, and dried it to make raisins. They also boiled the juice down into a thick syrup that was used as a sweetener. So the simple grape that Dionysus offered to his people was actually a prized part of their diet. It provided cherished sweetness and intoxication in the days before sugar and booze were overflowing from every grocery store.

At this point, you may be wondering why we've paired him with Posidaeja as his mother. That's because there's a whole set of myths about Dionysus that connect him with the sea, though most people aren't familiar with them. There are multiple variations, but the main story is that Dionysus was sailing in the Aegean when a bunch of pirates tried to take over his boat and sell him as a slave. In order to save himself from the attackers, he produced a variety of hallucinations that ranged from ivy and flute music to scary wild animals, depending on which version of the tale you read. These visions freaked out the sailors, who leapt overboard, turning into dolphins.

In MMP we interpret this set of myths to mean that Dionysus is a psychopomp for sailors who die at sea and others who are connected with the sea in various ways. The sea was incredibly important to the Minoans. They were surrounded by it on Crete and on every other island they visited. And they made their fortunes via the sea, traveling and trading in large, many-oared ships and fishing from smaller boats. They were an island people, so even the farmers had to acknowledge the sea as integral to their lives, shaping the weather that washed across the island.

We consider the dolphin to be one of Dionysus' symbols, possibly even a symbol for the spirits of the dead. Many cultures have long viewed the ocean as a gateway to the Underworld, where the souls of the deceased reside. It's probably no coincidence that Homer called the Aegean the wine-dark sea. If you've ever been out on the water at sunset, you know how the light drains away until it looks like you're floating on pure blackness. It's easy to see how people might have connected that with dark red wine and with a doorway that leads to the Underworld.

The grape harvest celebrations began early in Minoan culture and probably took place on farms and in vineyards. Later on, during palatial times, a practice developed around Dionysus' yearly rebirth at the Winter Solstice. This new addition to Dionysus' cult turned him into a solar year-king in addition to being a sacrificial harvest god. We don't know that he was necessarily the original deity whose birth was celebrated at Midwinter. In fact, we think that honor probably originally went to either Korydallos, the son of the Sun goddess who rebirths herself at Winter Solstice, or Tauros, whose mother Rhea is said to give birth in her sacred cave at that time of year. But the Mycenaeans appear to have taken quite a shine to Dionysus, calling him the "Cretan Zeus," so he got a bit of a promotion and a new set of myths while some of the other gods receded into the background.

Bear in mind, Minoan religion didn't stay the same during the many centuries of Minoan civilization. It changed and evolved over that time, adding layers as the culture shifted and evolved. Just like the layers of religion that developed over the centuries in Egypt and Mesopotamia, the people of Crete simply added the new festivals and rituals into their sacred calendar at the appropriate times on top of all the other stuff that was already there. In the last few centuries, the Mycenaeans probably had a certain amount of influence as well. So it's not as simple as saying, "Minoan religion was like this." It was a different thing at different times. For the purposes of our sacred calendar, as we celebrate it in the modern world, we've set Dionysus as the Divine Child born at the Winter Solstice.

The solar year-king symbology works well for Dionysus since he was already a dying-and-reborn god. Of course, gods don't really die, but they do descend to the Underworld and then return. And to a human, that looks like pretty much the same thing. Now, the solar year dies and is reborn at Winter Solstice, so we end up with two overlapping sets of rebirth and resurrection observances: one for the grape crop and one for the solar year. Since Dionysus was a god, not a human, he didn't have to conform to the laws of physics. Presumably this made sense to the people who worshiped him, because I doubt the grape harvest celebrations disappeared when the solar year mythos was added.

Let's have a look at the myths surrounding Dionysus' Midwinter birth. A number of caves on Crete were sacred to Rhea, and it's in one of these caves that she gave birth to Dionysus. Which cave was the 'real one' is a matter of debate today and was probably a hot topic in Minoan times, too. It was in this special cave that Rhea kept her infant son safe until he was old enough to go out. While he was there, the goat-goddess Amalthea fed him on goat's milk and the Melissae fed him honey. He was also attended by the Kouretes who drummed, danced, and stamped their feet. The legends say they did this either to drown out the infant Dionysus' cries (in other words, to keep him hidden) or to entertain him, depending on which source you read. The fact that the Kouretes drummed and danced suggests a tradition that engaged in ecstatic and shamanic rites.

Above all else, Dionysus is an ecstatic god of epiphany—the revelation of the divine to humanity. One of his names in Greek times was Eleutherios (literally, 'the liberator'). The etymology of this word is related to Eileithyia, the midwife-goddess whose name means 'the deliverer' (see her entry below). The ecstatic journeys that Dionysus' devotees undertook helped liberate them from ordinary consciousness and bring them transcendent visions of the sacred. They may have felt reborn, which would explain the connection with Eileithyia. During Dionysiac rites, intoxication was considered to be a sign of possession by the god. Wine, of course, helped his followers achieve these altered states of consciousness. It's likely that other substances were added to the wine as well. Though ivy was one of Dionysus' mind-altering plants in Greek times, the favored ingredient in Minoan times was more likely opium, extracted from the poppies the Minoans grew.

In later Greek times, Dionysus' main emblem was the thyrsus, a fennel stalk topped with a pinecone and sometimes wound around with ivy. The pinecone is a reminder that he has long been closely associated with trees, especially pines and firs. It's also a phallic symbol. Some tales say that, instead of being born in a cave, Dionysus was born beneath a fir tree while a special star shone brightly in the sky above. It's likely that Dionysus' pine or fir tree is the shamanic World Tree, the one that connects the Upperworld and the Underworld and allows the god (and the shaman) to move between them.

Speaking of fir trees, the silver fir (*Abies alba*) was particularly sacred to Dionysus. Its resin, a turpentine-like oil, was used in ancient Crete as well as by the later Greeks as a wine additive. It added flavor and also helped the wine keep longer without spoiling. This beverage is the ancestor of the modern-day Greek wine retsina.

Dionysus was also associated with bees and beehives. This connection has a two-fold significance. First, honey and beeswax were added to the wine in Dionysiac rites both for flavor and to enhance the intoxicating effects. And second, bees and beehives were associated with the Underworld and the Ancestors. The Melissae cared for the souls of the dead in the Underworld; the Minoans may have built their tombs in the shape of beehives as a reminder of this symbology. So this underscores Dionysus' identity as a shamanic deity and psychopomp.

In classical Greek times, Dionysus' female worshipers were called maenads and were depicted as a procession of drunken revelers singing, dancing, and parading around behind the god. These figures were probably created from the nymphs or nature spirits who were part of Dionysus' original divine retinue, combined with his worshipers who took part in ecstatic rites (serious religious practices, not wild parties). Dionysus' association with the grapevine and the sea makes him a nature god of sorts, so it makes sense that he would be surrounded by nature spirits. It's interesting that as late as classical times, the male nature spirits in Dionysus' retinue (satyrs and sileni, for instance) were still depicted as semi-divine creatures while the female nature spirits had been 'demoted' to mere drunken women.

If you'd like to include Dionysus in your sacred space, some obvious possibilities include all the forms of grapes: grape juice, wine, fresh grapes, raisins. You could also use dried grapevines as a decoration. They're easy to find in craft shops in the form of wreaths or in bundles for making your own craft projects. Or you could focus on the trees in the legends and include pinecones, branches of fir or pine, or artwork that depicts pine trees and pinecones. You could also include images or figurines of dolphins to emphasize Dionysus' connection with the sea as a gateway to the Underworld and the Ancestors. Triton or conch shells, especially when used as trumpets to signal the beginning or end of ritual, are also a good choice for him.

There are plenty of Dionysus figurines available from online sources and local shops, if you'd like that kind of image on your altar. Some are copies of Greek and Roman sculptures, and some are modern interpretations. Dionysus has long been a favorite subject of painters, so artistic depictions of him abound. For many people, deep purple and deep green evoke his presence, so using altar cloths and accessories in these colors can also help you key into his energy. Interestingly, these aren't just the colors of the grapevine, but also of the sea as the Sun sets.

The most obvious offering you can make to Dionysus is wine, red or white or even retsina. He doesn't generally like distilled liquor, but he adores brewed alcoholic beverages. Do be careful, though, with the stranger modern flavored ones; sometimes he decides he doesn't like ones with certain herbs, fruits, or other flavorings. Interestingly, he will also generally accept offerings of homemade red wine vinegar, but not the store-bought stuff. If you'd like to dedicate an activity to him, offerings of singing and dancing will do nicely—and intoxication isn't required. Speaking of intoxication, if you're a teetotaler, you can offer him purple grape juice and he'll happily accept it. But don't expect to get away with offering him grape juice if you drink alcohol, even if you're temporarily "dry" (such as during a pregnancy).

As with offerings, wine is also an excellent method for divination with Dionysus' aid, and I don't mean drinking until you see things! But filling a bowl or wide cup with some dark red wine and scrying in it works quite well. This is best done in low light like candlelight or outdoors at sunset.

If you'll be embodying Dionysus in ritual, the main thing to remember is that he isn't a wild-and-crazy party god. This is religion, not a parody of it. You'll want to dress in a way that evokes the slightly more civilized side of the ancient world, since viticulture, winemaking, and reaching ecstatic states are sophisticated skills. You could try a simple kilt like Minoan men wore, or you could go for something that looks more like later

Greek or Roman clothing. A wreath of ivy around your head wouldn't be amiss, or perhaps a cluster of grapes drawn on your cheek or shoulder with face paint. Remember, above all, that Dionysus offers ecstasy not so we can escape the darker parts of life, but so we can embrace them.

The Horned Ones

This family of deities demonstrates how difficult it can be to tease out the details of individual gods and goddesses in the Minoan pantheon, and how they begin to look more like reflections and reweavings of each other than human-style relatives. Some of these deities survived into later Greek mythology: the Minotaur, Europa, Amalthea, and Britomartis. Their stories in Greek myth are well known but are not always flattering. After all, the Greeks wanted to make themselves look good, and an easy way to do that was to make the Minoans look bad. The Greeks weren't necessarily awful people. This kind of rewriting of myth is common throughout human history as cultures overtake each other. Focusing on the Horned Ones as we believe they were in Minoan times gives us a very different impression than the Greek stories do.

First of all, in MMP the Horned Ones come in pairs based on the type of animals they represent. The Minotaur and Europa are bovine (bull/cow) deities; the Minocapros and Amalthea are goat deities; and the Minelathos and Britomartis are the stag and the deer. They all appear to be associated in one way or another with the Moon. This was a common connection in the ancient world where the horns of the Moon (the Moon in its crescent phase) and the horns of animals were interchangeable symbols. We think there may have been an ibex (wild goat) pair of Horned Ones early on, in contrast to the domesticated goats called agrimi that sometimes go feral but aren't truly wild. But the ibex appears to have receded from the spotlight over the centuries, and we're left with the three pairs of Horned Ones I listed above.

In addition to the other layers of meaning that the sacred horns have, we associate them with the Horned Ones. The sacred horns are most strongly connected with the Minotaur and Europa, given that they look most closely like cow or bull horns, but they can be used to symbolize the other Horned Ones as well.

Based on the artwork that's been found at various locations on Crete, it looks like different versions of the Horned Ones were honored from one place to another. For instance, the bull/cow pair was prominent at Knossos and the stag/deer pair appears to have been worshiped at Phaistos. There are representations of goats on artwork from several peak sanctuaries, so the goat versions of the Horned Ones were probably honored there. These may simply be regional variations that go back to different totemic animal deities from very early times on Crete. But they may also have to do with the astronomical qualities of the Moon that were important in each location. The Minoan astronomers kept track of details like the southernmost and northernmost places where the Moon rises along the horizon as well as the phases of the lunar cycle. For instance, some peak sanctuaries are oriented to the southernmost moonrise and others aren't. In a sense, even 'official' Minoan religion was pretty individualistic, with each region having its own flavor and practice.

There are some interesting seal stones from late Minoan times that show male figures that are half human and half animal, specifically bull, stag, and goat. Dance ethnography research suggests that a shapeshifting spiritual practice arose during that era, and that may have influenced the way later people envisioned the Minotaur and the other Minoan horned gods. Conventional images of the Minotaur show him with a man's body and a bull's head. All three of the horned gods can be envisioned as half-human (or human-like, anyway, since they're gods) and half-animal or animal-headed. But you can also imagine them as divine animals or as anthropomorphic beings. In contrast, the horned goddesses tended to be described as fully human in appearance in the fragments of myth that made it through to classical times, though there are some hints that they may have had animal forms as well. Just remember, even if you're imagining them as looking human, they're not human at all.

The Minotaur and Europa

The Minotaur

Pronunciation: MIH-*noe-tor*

Epithets: Moon-Bull

Europa

Pronunciation: you-ROE-*pah*

Epithets: Moon-Cow, Pasiphaë (PAH-sih-fay-ee, her doublet or twin)

Let's start with the most famous set of Horned Ones: the Minotaur and Europa. You've probably already guessed that to the Minoans, the Minotaur wasn't an evil monster. Instead, he was a revered god. And his female counterpart, the Moon-Cow we know as Europa, wasn't the victim of abduction and rape like the Greeks told it. Instead, she was the honored goddess who may have been the Minotaur's consort or even a female version of him. As I mentioned in the section about Ariadne, the Greek tale of Theseus and the Minotaur really has nothing to do with the ancient Minoans. The Greek culture-hero Theseus appeared centuries after the downfall of Minoan civilization, and his adventures in Crete were added to his repertory of stories very late in the game, so the Minoans never even heard of him.

Before we get too far into our discussion of the bovine Horned Ones, let's talk a little about horns. I've noticed that in a lot of history and art books, images of cattle with horns are automatically labeled as bulls. Now, if there are bullish bits of genitalia dangling below, or if the image has the heavy shoulder muscling and thick neck of a bull, then it's pretty clearly a bull. But did you know that in ancient times all cattle, both male and female, had horns? It's true. Then in the late 19th and early 20th centuries, farmers and ranchers started keeping their cattle penned up in crowded conditions instead of just out on the open prairie.

In close quarters, those horns can do a lot of damage, even accidentally. So the farmers and ranchers removed the horns or horn buds while the animals were still young. This process is called polling. They even bred cattle that never grew horns (these are called polled breeds) so the animals wouldn't injure each other with their sharp-and-pointy bits. In modern times, bulls and steers that are raised for show or as trained animals for the movies often have their horns left intact, giving people the impression that only bulls have horns. But the fact is, when we see images of horned cattle from ancient Crete, unless we can tell from the genitalia or the body shape that the animal is male, we simply can't make that assumption. The Moon-Cow has horns just like the Moon-Bull does, and just like some modern heritage breeds of cattle do (Scottish Highland cattle, for instance).

So let's get back to our Horned Ones. What have we figured out about the original Minoan version of the Minotaur, other than the fact that he has something to do with bulls? Actually, his identity as a bull gives us a clue: he's connected with our other bull gods, Tauros Asterion and Zagreus. In MMP, we consider the three to be different faces of the same god. So the Minotaur is a shamanic god who has access to the Underworld. The Minotaur does what all shamanic gods do when they descend to the World Below and then return: he helps us find renewal, leave behind the stuff that no longer serves us, and be reborn in our own lives.

The Greeks put the Minotaur at the center of the Labyrinth, but they called him a monster. If we look more closely at the imagery and think about what the labyrinth journey represents, we can see that he can help us access the dark and shadowy parts of ourselves—our own inner monster, if you will. The shadows within us aren't evil, but they can be scary. The Minotaur is a powerful being who can protect us during that journey and help us face our fears.

Since he's associated with the Labyrinth, by definition the he has a relationship with Ariadne. In the Greek story, Ariadne is just a girl with a ball of string, and the Minotaur is a man-eating monster. But we know Ariadne is really a goddess, and the Minotaur is no monster. Brother and sister, both children of Rhea (remember, the Minotaur is a face of Tauros Asterion), the two of them work together to help us navigate our own inner darkness, our internal Underworld, and find healing.

The famous bull leaping and cattle sacrifice activities that we see throughout Minoan art were probably associated with the Minotaur, Tauros Asterion, and/or Zagreus, since they're the bull gods. In fact, the part in the Greek story about Theseus slaying the Minotaur may have been the remnant of a bull sacrifice ritual from ancient Crete. Throughout the ancient world, athletic contests were typically held at the funerals of great kings and heroes as well as at the yearly recognition of the "death" (descent to the Underworld) of a god. These are called funeral games, and the bull leaping may have been part of the funeral celebration of the Minoan bull-god.

What about Europa? She's a doublet or twin of Pasiphaë, another cow-goddess with similar attributes. In MMP, Europa is the name we use most of the time, but some of us prefer Pasiphaë. Either one works just fine. We don't know her Minoan name, but we know she's the Moon-Cow, the bearer of life-giving milk. There's a lot of breast and udder symbolism in Minoan art. This shows us how important the mothering and nurturing aspects of the goddess were to the Minoans. Unlike the Minotaur, Europa is always shown as fully human in Greek mythology. But the part of the Greek story when she hides in a mechanical cow in order to mate with a bull suggests that she also had a Minoan version in which she took the form of a cow.

Europa is connected with the Minoans because the Greeks cast her as King Minos' mother (see the section about Minos below— he was really a god, not a human king). It's possible that she was originally a Levantine goddess, since she's described as being Phoenician or coming from that region. Her doublet/twin Pasiphaë is also called a queen of Crete in Greek mythology, but she, too was said to have come from a foreign land, in her case Colchis on the shore of the Black Sea. Wherever these goddesses came from, like Antheia, they found a home on Crete.

The etymology of Europa's name, which means 'broad face' or 'wide eye,' tells us that she was connected with the Moon, particularly the full Moon. Interestingly, though, she and her double/twin Pasiphaë may originally have been Sun goddesses.

Dance ethnography and comparative mythology suggest that, like Artemis, both Europa and Pasiphaë were originally faces of the Mediterranean Sun goddess in the Bronze Age. They appear to have been changed to Moon goddesses during the Bronze Age collapse and/or the shift into the Iron Age soon afterward. Since we already have a Minoan Sun goddess in Therasia, in MMP we've chosen to continue associating Europa with the Moon, in keeping with the rest of the Horned Ones.

Of course, Europa is always associated with cattle. The Greek version of the tale says that Zeus was so enamored with her that he turned himself into a white bull and hung out in the herd of cattle that Europa's family owned. He was so tame that she petted him and even got onto his back, at which point he sprang up and flew with her to Crete, where he raped her. As a number of scholars have pointed out, this story is probably a later Greek misinterpretation of the divine marriage of a bull-god and cow-goddess. In other words, it wasn't a Hellenic Greek abduction and rape, but a Minoan-era mating of the divine pair.

The Greek version of the story also gives us a clue about a flower that was probably sacred to Europa: the crocus. According to the classical Greek poet Hesiod, Zeus saw Europa gathering flowers in a springtime meadow. Not only did he change himself into a bull; he also breathed a magical crocus from his mouth to entice her to come over to him. When she did, he grabbed her, and away he went. So we can count crocuses among Europa's symbols as well. Bear in mind, this isn't the saffron crocus that's sacred to Therasia. The saffron crocus is unusual in that it blooms in the autumn. Most crocuses bloom in the spring, and that's the kind we associate with Europa.

If you'd like to include the Minotaur and Europa in your sacred space, you have a variety of options, depending on which symbols appeal to you. You might first want to decide whether you want to focus on just one or the other or both of them together, then choose your altar furnishings accordingly. To begin with, the sacred horns could represent either one or both of them. You could also include any kind of bull or cow imagery you like.

Rhytons in the shape of cow's heads aren't as easy to find now as they were in ancient Crete, but some housewares shops sell little porcelain cream pitchers in the shape of a cow, and that's pretty close. You can also find artwork and figurines in the shape of bulls, cows, and realistic horns.

If you're comfortable using animal parts in your sacred space, you could include items made from cowhide, bone, or horns to honor the Minotaur, Europa, or both of them. If the conventional depiction of the Minotaur appeals to you, you could include artwork or figurines of the half-man, half-bull version. And if you're specifically honoring the Minotaur, you could also include a labyrinth on your altar, since that's his domain as well as Ariadne's.

Colors that evoke the feeling of these two deities include natural shades of brown and tan and possibly black and cream, the colors you'd find in a herd of cattle. If the Minotaur and Europa also suggest the Moon to you, you could include lunar symbols in your sacred space, especially the crescent Moon. Of course, horns of any kind — the stylized sacred horns or realistic ones — can be Moon symbols as well as animal ones. And Europa has long been associated with the full Moon, so that's a possibility, too.

The usual offering to any of the Horned Ones is red wine, the darker, the better. Even though they're animal gods and the Minoans practiced animal sacrifice, we've found that it's not a good idea to offer them meat. They often react very negatively to meat offerings, so we don't recommend it. Europa will also accept offerings of cow's milk (whole milk, please, not lowfat or skim, and definitely not goat's milk or plant-based milks like soy or almond).

All the Horned Ones are amenable to divination with bones, both literal and figurative. You can collect animal bones from meals or from road kill (please use all appropriate health and safety precautions) or buy them from reputable dealers. A set of bones for divination can also include items that aren't made of bone, such as stones. The Horned Ones seem to prefer either natural pebbles and rocks that you've found outdoors or polished stones in shades of brown, tan, and cream. Though some sets of bones may include other items such as seashells or metal tokens, those are not good choices for bones you'll be using with the Horned Ones. You could, however, include small carved stone cow or bull figurines for divination with the Minotaur and Europa. And of course, a piece of cowhide would be an appropriate casting "cloth."

If you'll be embodying the Minotaur or Europa in ritual, decide first how you want people to see the deity: in human form, half-human and half-bovine, or fully animal. A cow or bull mask is probably the easiest way to present yourself as one of these deities. The rest of your clothing should be simple or rough and primitive in shades of brown and tan. It doesn't have to be leather, but it shouldn't look tailored or modern.

The Minocapros and Amalthea

The Minocapros
Pronunciation: mee-noe-CAP-ros
Epithets: Moon-Goat, Wild One, Mountain Climber
Amalthea
Pronunciation: ah-MAL-thee-ah
Epithets: Adrasteia (ah-DRAH-stee-ah), Ida (ee-DAH),
Adamanthea (ah-dah-MAN-thee-ah), Dikte (DEEK-tay,
DEEK-tee)

I find it interesting that, out of all the male Horned Ones, only the bull-god held onto his name down to Greek times. It looks like the Greeks latched onto the bull cult pretty vigorously but weren't nearly as interested in the goat or stag cults, maybe because the bull cult was still 'big' in the Levant and Mesopotamia by the time the Greeks came around. So while we still know Amalthea's name, we can't be sure what the Minoans called their goat-god. Minocapros is a term that was coined in Victorian times for the Moon-Goat.

While bulls and cows are the predominant Horned Ones, we also find a lot of goats in Minoan art, so we know they were important. The agrimi or kri-kri is the local name for the domesticated goat on Crete that has gone feral in places. The males have long, curving horns, while the females have much shorter horns that curve very little, if at all. The frescoes and other artwork show these goats cavorting around the mountains, suggesting that the goat deities were revered at the peak sanctuaries on Crete as well as being associated with the wild mountain areas. It's possible that the Minocapros is a relative of the well-known goat-god Pan, who was probably prancing through the hills and mountains of Greece long before the Indo-Europeans got there.

We don't know for sure how the Minoans envisioned the Minocapros. They may have pictured him as a deity who could change form, from man to goat and back again. Or he may have been a half-goat, half-human creature in much the same way that the Minotaur is half-bull and half-man. As I mentioned above, there are seal stones from late Minoan times showing shapeshifting beings that are half-man and half-goat, so if that kind of image has meaning for you, use it.

Like cattle, goats were domesticated animals in ancient Crete. The kri-kri or agrimi is actually a feral animal, having gone wild from the ancient domesticated herds on the island. So goats were familiar livestock to the Minoans. The people of ancient Crete relied on them for meat, milk, and hides. In other words, domesticated goats were a source of sustenance and life, just like cattle. But given what we can see from Minoan artwork, there were plenty of wild or feral goats in ancient Crete, too, so the goat-gods straddle the line between domesticated and wild.

In MMP we view the goat-god as a shamanic, Underworld-traveling god just like the Minotaur. We know that animal sacrifice was common in ancient Crete. The real death of the animal would have represented the symbolic death of the god as he traveled to the World Below. The Hagia Triada sarcophagus clearly shows two goats underneath the table that holds a sacrificial bull. Just like the rest of the ancient world, the Minoans sacrificed animals as a ritual act in which the animal embodied the deity.

But what about the goat-goddess? Amalthea plays a major role in the tale of Dionysus' birth to Rhea: she's the source of the milk that sustains the infant Dionysus while he's hidden in Rhea's cave. In other words, Amalthea is Dionysus' wet-nurse. We don't know how early or late this layer of the story was added to the mythology—Minoan myth is a complex, many-layered thing—but this may be a way of showing Dionysus being adopted by the goat-god. This is similar to the tale that developed many centuries later about the mythical founders of Rome, Romulus and Remus, who were nursed by a she-wolf (the totemic animal-god of Rome).

We don't know nearly as much about Amalthea as we do about Europa, but there's still a lot we can figure out from the tidbits the Greeks left us. First of all, Amalthea's position as Dionysus' foster-mother is reinforced by the Greek tale of her being Zeus' foster-mother—remember, the Greeks called Dionysus "Cretan Zeus." That name was eventually shortened to just Zeus, confusing the stories even more. Amalthea is also associated with the names Dikte and Ida, two mountains on Crete where there are caves sacred to Rhea.

In some versions of the Greek myth, Amalthea is also called Adrasteia or Adamanthea. These names give us more clues about Amalthea's personality and identity. The name Adrasteia means 'inescapable,' in other words, the one who kept Dionysus completely safe in that cave. And Adrasteia is called the sister or double of Ida, the nymph (demoted goddess) of Mt. Ida, so we're back to the cave again. Adrasteia is also one of Rhea's epithets, which points us back toward the fun-house of mirrors that makes the Minoan pantheon so interesting. And the name Adamanthea means 'untamable goddess,' suggesting that the goat-goddess is a little on the wild side!

Like Europa, Amalthea is a giver of nourishment and life—she provides milk for the infant Dionysus. But there's more to her generosity than just that. It's her horn that created the original cornucopia, the magical Horn of Plenty from which all things come. The Greeks said that the infant Zeus (who would be Dionysus in the original Minoan version of the story) didn't know his own strength and accidentally broke off one of Amalthea's horns when he was playing with her, creating the cornucopia. Personally, I think the goddess gives of her bounty voluntarily and doesn't need anyone to break one of her horns off, but that's just my opinion.

Like Europa, Amalthea is always shown as either fully human or fully goat and never half-and-half. In the story of Dionysus' birth and infancy, she appears to shift back and forth from one to the other with ease. So you could think of her as a goddess or a totemic animal spirit, or both.

If you'd like to include the Minocapros and Amalthea in your sacred space, as with the other Horned Ones, first you need to decide whether you're going to honor one or the other or both. Of course, the sacred horns are always appropriate for the Horned Ones. And any kind of representation of goats or goat horns would work, too, whether it's from Minoan art or something more modern. Cornucopias are also appropriate for Amalthea. If you can find a figurine of a goddess holding a cornucopia, it will work just fine as long as you satisfy two criteria: no other deity name is painted or embossed on the statue, and the cornucopia is full of something like fruits and vegetables rather than coins (figurines of the Roman goddess Fortuna often include coins pouring out of the cornucopia, and coins hadn't been invented yet in Minoan times). As for the Minocapros, artwork or figurines of fauns or Pan-type figures could work as long as they don't include any other deity's name painted or embossed on them.

If you're comfortable using animal parts, you could include items made of goat hide or horns in your sacred space. As for colors, the natural tones of cream, grey, tan, black, and brown of the goat herd would work well here. The goat-deities are associated with the Moon, so you could include lunar images in your sacred space. Animal horns suggest the crescent Moon, but given the wild nature of the goat-y types, including their later incarnations as fauns, I think the full Moon also would be very appropriate here.

Just like with the other Horned Ones, red wine is an appropriate offering for Amalthea and the Minocapros. Amalthea also appreciates offerings of goat's milk and cheese. As with the other Horned Ones, please don't offer meat to either of these deities.

As I noted in the section about the Minotaur and Europa, all the Horned Ones seem to like the use of bones for divination. A set of bones can include real bones—goat knucklebones are particularly appropriate here if you can get them—but they can also include other small objects as well. As with the bovine Horned Ones, avoid seashells and metal items, but stones of all sorts will work, including those carved into various shapes. The Minocapros and Amalthea both like brightly colored stones as well as those with earthier tones. A piece of goat hide or chamois or the goat hide head of a drum would be a good surface for casting your bones on.

If you'll be embodying either of the goat Horned Ones, decide first how you want to present them in the ritual. You don't have to go full-on "Pan" for the Minocapros. Simple horns of the type that are easily found at costume shops and the Ren faire, plus rustic clothing in shades of brown and tan will work just fine. The Minocapros seems especially happy to have his embodying clergy be barefoot, but of course you should pay attention to your own safety given the setting for the ritual. Embodying Amalthea can be as simple as dressing in old-fashioned rustic clothing like a storybook goatherd might wear. She seems to enjoy flowers very much, in the hair or as a necklace, though I suspect a real goat would eat them! If it's appropriate to the ritual, you could also carry a cornucopia.

The Minelathos and Britomartis

Minelathos

Pronunciation: mih-nee-LAH-thos

Epithets: Moon-Deer, Moon-Stag

Britomartis

Pronunciation: bree-TOE-mar-tees (that's the ancient Greek
pronunciation; modern Greek pronunciation turns the B
into a V sound)

Epithets: Diktynna (deek-TIN-ah), Lady of the Beasts, The
Huntress

The stag-and-deer pair of the Minelathos and Britomartis are a little different from the other Horned Ones. First of all, deer were never a livestock animal on Crete, either in the ancient world or in modern times, as far as we can tell. So these are completely wild Horned Ones, not tame at all. And second, Britomartis isn't just a female Horned One but a huntress as well, at least according to the Hellenic Greeks. So let's see what we can figure out about these two deities.

We know very little about the Minelathos except the few remnants that survived into Greek times. Like the Minocapros, we don't know what his original Minoan name was. If we're looking for clues in later mythology, the Greek legendary hero Actaeon is probably an echo or relative of the original Minoan stag-god. In his story, he sees Artemis (the Greek version of Britomartis) bathing nude in a pool in the woods. She becomes enraged at this slight, turns him into a stag, and hunts him to death. This tale suggests that, like the other Horned Ones, the Minelathos is a sacrificial or shamanic god, slain by the goddess or her earthly representative, the priestess.

We can't be certain which types of deer lived on Crete in Minoan times. There aren't any left on the island today. They were all hunted and killed off. But we do know there were roe deer, because bones have been found where people roasted and ate the meat. And a fresco fragment from Hagia Triada shows a pair of fallow deer being led to sacrifice. It's likely there were a lot more wild animals, especially large ones, on Crete before the invention of hunting rifles than there are now. So I suspect deer were probably a common sight in the countryside during Minoan times, and the people would have felt that these Horned Ones were constantly present among them.

We know a lot more about Britomartis than about her consort because the Greeks apparently found her fascinating. Her name, which isn't native Greek and may originally come from the Minoan language, means 'sweet maiden' or 'sweet virgin.' This is the type of epithet that was often used to pacify fearsome or dangerous deities. It's appropriate for Britomartis, since she appears to have been a fierce huntress. As usual, the Greeks demoted her from a goddess to a nymph and had her become one of Artemis' followers. But she was originally a full-fledged goddess very similar to Artemis, complete with her associations with the Moon, hunting, and deer.

Britomartis is also known as Diktynna or Dikte, names that connect her with Rhea's sacred mountain and cave. So, like Amalthea, Britomartis is associated with Rhea and her birthing-cave, though we don't know for sure exactly what her role was in that story. She's shown on Cretan coins from Greek times, several centuries later than the Minoans, as one of Zeus' (Dionysus') wet-nurses. This suggests that she originally played a similar role to Amalthea with the infant Dionysus. We also know that the Greeks associated her with mountains in general as well as Mt. Dikte in particular. As early as Homer's time, the Greeks called her Potnia Theron: Mistress of the Animals. And, like Artemis, she was associated with the Moon, especially the full Moon.

Her connection with mountains makes sense in two ways. First, Rhea's birthing-cave is set in the side of a sacred mountain, with a peak sanctuary on top to emphasize that sacredness. So Britomartis' role as the infant Dionysus' wet-nurse connects her with the sacred mountains of Crete. And second, the deer of ancient Crete lived in the wild areas of the island (remember, they weren't livestock), and the mountainous regions of Crete are about as wild as it gets.

There's more to Britomartis than just mountains, though. Some confusion about the meaning of her name eventually led to another association for this goddess: the sea. This misunderstanding has to do with her epithet Diktynna. Of course, it refers to Mt. Dikte on Crete, but by the time the Hellenic Greeks came around, she was worshiped in several places around the Mediterranean, and apparently her original connection with Mt. Dikte had been forgotten. The Greeks saw that her name looked a lot like their word for hunting nets (diktya) and decided that she was the Lady of the Nets. Somehow from the idea of nets came the story that she was fleeing King Minos' advances on Crete and leaped into some fishermen's nets. The fishermen then carried her to safety in mainland Greece.

Of course, this story is really a mythical explanation for how Diktynna's worship spread from Crete to other locations. We know Minos was a god, not a king. And given the way we think Minoan society worked in terms of respect for women, I seriously doubt one of their gods would have chased after a goddess the way Zeus did so often in Greek myth. But this is an excellent example of how mythology can get twisted around when the original meanings have been lost and people in a different culture do their best to make something meaningful out of the few remaining bits.

Still, the connection with the sea is interesting since the sea and the Moon are close comrades in mythology around the world, and the Horned Ones are all associated with the Moon. The link with nets also suggests that by the time the Greeks collected up the stories about Britomartis, she was considered a huntress in general and not just a huntress of deer. Nets were used to catch small prey like birds, not big animals like deer. For deer hunting, the Minoans probably used spears and possibly bows and arrows.

As with the other Horned Ones, if you want to include the Minelathos and Britomartis in your sacred space, you could start with the sacred horns. Personally, I find the stylized horns to be not so great a match for the deer gods because deer antlers don't look quite like cow or goat horns, but if the symbolism works for you, then use it. The Minoans apparently did. Of course, you could also use any kind of deer imagery, like artwork and figurines. If you're comfortable using animal parts in your sacred space, deer antlers are a good choice here. They can often be found in pet stores for a very low price—they're sold as chew toys for dogs! And since antlers are shed naturally every year, this is one animal product you can include, knowing that no harm has come to the animal in the process.

Natural colors like shades of tan and brown work well for the Minelathos and Britomartis. You can even key the colors to the type of deer you'd like to focus on. Roe deer have a slightly reddish color, and fallow deer are a light tan with cream-colored spots (even the adults have the spots, not just the babies). I find imagery of deer hoofprints to be especially evocative for this pair, so if that calls to you, consider using artwork or photos of hoofprints. I've even seen small sculptures that were essentially plaster casts of deer hoofprints, as if the deer had walked across the ground and you had that piece of the Earth to put on your altar.

Just as with the other Horned Ones, the Minelathos and Britomartis appreciate offerings of red wine. They're the wildest of the Horned Ones, and they especially like to have wild land dedicated to them, even if it's just a small corner of your yard. It should be a place that's not cultivated or pruned in any way, but just left to its own devices. You can pour out libations of red wine to them in that place and listen for them to speak to you.

Like the other two pairs of Horned Ones, the Minelathos and Britomartis are happy to help with divination using a set of bones. But unlike the others, they seem to prefer only actual bones combined with natural pebbles and stones—no fancy polished ones from a rock shop. They also like interesting bits of wood and tiny pinecones included in the bones set. So go on a walk in the forest and see what you can find that might work. A piece of deer hide is your best choice for a casting cloth, but if that's too hard to find, chamois also works well.

These two are the wildest of the Horned Ones, so if you're embodying them in ritual, bear that in mind. Antlers are appropriate for both the Minelathos and Britomartis. No, female deer don't have antlers, but the huntress and the hunted become one during the chase. Face paint and very primitive clothing are good choices. Go barefoot if that's a safe thing to do given your ritual space.

Serpent Mother

Epithets: Basilissa *(bah-see-LEE-sah—this is the ancient Greek pronunciation; modern Greek has a V sound instead of the B at the beginning of her name), Snake Goddess*

The Serpent Mother is one of the most enigmatic deities we have, even though the Snake Goddess figurines are among the most iconic representations of Minoan religion. In the ancient Mediterranean, snakes were associated with grain deities because they prey on the rodents that eat the stored grain. The Minoan temples had large quantities of wheat and barley stored in pithoi (tall ceramic vases) and small stone silos. The people relied on this grain not just for sharing during public feasting, but also in case the crops failed. Protecting the grain, then, was vital to ensuring the stability of Minoan society. So from a simple agricultural perspective, you could consider the Serpent Mother to be an aspect of Rhea or Ariadne or both, a protector of the grain crop. But there's more to her than that.

There are some interesting perforated vessels decorated with snakes that have been found at Minoan archaeological sites. These containers have holes in them like the ones from Neolithic Old Europe that were apparently used for rain-making rituals (the water pours through the holes, imitating rain, as a form of sympathetic magic). So we can associate the Serpent Mother with rain as well: the hissing of the rain as it falls, the lightning snaking through the sky.

Many of us also feel that the Serpent Mother is connected with Ourania, our cosmic or universal mother goddess. Once again we see how the Minoan pantheon can look like a carnival fun house full of mirrors more than a human-style family tree. There's a sense in which we can view the Underworld as an upside-down version of the cosmos. Think of an Earth-centric view in which the daytime sky is above and the Underworld is below. Then as the Sun sets in the evening and slides beneath the Earth, the Underworld slides up overhead: the starry night sky. Nighttime is daytime in reverse, so to speak. Then at dawn, the Underworld retreats below the Earth again, chased away by the growing light from the Sun. So the Underworld is beneath everything, holding it all up, completing the circle (or the sphere, if you like). This idea brings us back around to grain, since the grain grows out of the ground, coming up from underneath as a gift from the ancestors who reside in the Underworld.

Our interactions with the Serpent Mother make it clear that she's an Underworld goddess, among other things. On a very basic level, we can think of snakes as emerging from holes in the ground, something they do regularly in the natural world. A surprising number of people have had visions associated with her, in which a room full of writhing snakes resolves itself into a labyrinth design on the floor. That suggests a strong connection with Ariadne, specifically in her Underworld aspect. The Serpent Mother can help you plumb the depths of your own shadows and is a valuable guide in the labyrinth, either on her own or alongside Ariadne and the Minotaur.

In addition to emotional healing through labyrinth work, the Serpent Mother can also be addressed for physical healing. It's probably her snake that ended up on Asclepius' rod, which isn't the same as Hermes' caduceus. Many of us consider the healer-god Paean (also spelled Paeon), whose name is attested in the Linear B tablets, to be the Serpent Mother's son. And it's his name that eventually became one of Asclepius' epithets. That's all a bit tangled, but it all points back to the Serpent Mother, whom we can ask for help with healing of all sorts. She's patient and compassionate, but she also expects us to put in the effort on our end when we ask her for assistance with healing. In other words, getting better might involve facing issues you've been avoiding thinking about. But it will be worth it in the end, and the Serpent Mother can help you find the strength to work your way toward wholeness.

The most obvious way to start an altar to the Serpent Mother is with a Snake Goddess figurine. Reproductions of the two famous figurines from Knossos are pretty easy to find online and in metaphysical shops. The Snake Goddess figurine with her arms raised was originally painted red and yellow. Those are good colors to center on when you're designing your altar if you want to focus on the agricultural and grain aspects of the Serpent Mother, since the yellow is the ripe grain and the red is the rich Earth that it grows from. Of course, snake images and art of all kinds are appropriate, though you should stick with non-venomous types (there are no venomous snakes on Crete). You could also include grain, such as stalks of wheat. And if you want to include the Serpent Mother's more cosmic aspect, I recommend visionary art that includes both snake images and the dark starry sky. For the cosmic or Underworld aspect of the Serpent Mother, concentrate on deep, dark colors like navy blue, very dark purple, and black.

The Serpent Mother accepts offerings of water, wine, and grain. She isn't usually interested in offerings of food or flowers, but she does enjoy resiny incense (myrrh, frankincense, copal, labdanum). She also accepts offerings of volunteer work on projects whose aim is healing, such as HIV awareness, or hunger, such as soup kitchens. If you're not sure whether the work you want to offer her is appropriate, spend some time in meditation with her and find out. If what you were thinking of won't work, she might be able to give you some ideas for something she'll accept.

Divination with the Serpent Mother can be very insightful. You can call on her to aid you with almost any kind of divination you might normally do, including ones you don't usually think of as Minoan (Tarot and oracle cards, for instance, though I will put in a plug here for my Minoan Tarot deck). She is also happy to assist with scrying and pendulum work, as well as simple meditation for solutions to your problem.

The easiest way to embody the Serpent Mother in ritual is to dress in a simplified version of the Snake Goddess figurine's outfit—a long, sweeping skirt and close-fitting short sleeved top. A scarf wrapped around your waist as a belt can finish the look. You could go for the Grain Goddess aspect by dressing in shades of red and yellow, or the Cosmic/Underworld Goddess aspect by dressing in deep and dark colors. You'll need two snakes, one for each hand: rubber ones, please, unless you happen to have a couple of very cooperative live ones at your disposal, and of course, always treat them with great care and respect.

Zagreus

Pronunciation: zah-GROOS

Epithets: The Dismembered One, The Goodly Bull, The Bull Who Comes Wreathed in Flowers in the Spring

One of Tauros' other names that's especially important in terms of his status as a shamanic god is Zagreus. No one is really sure what his name means, but a couple of popular etymologies include 'the goodly bull' and 'the dismembered one.' Not to be confused with the Greek Zeus, Zagreus is a much older god whose rites may have involved the sacrifice and dismemberment of animals, either wild or domestic. The concept of dismemberment is important in shamanism. The spiritworker must be taken apart and put back together again in the course of ecstatic journeys in order to gain new knowledge and understanding. But dismemberment also happens when a bull is sacrificed and then carved up to be cooked (the ancients didn't waste food, though they did give the gods their due).

Zagreus is often identified with a bull, possibly because it was bulls or bull calves that were sacrificed to him. Or it may be that bulls or calves were sacrificed to him because he was a bull-god. That sort of detail is hard to tease out from so many centuries away. In Minoan art we find images of bulls participating in parades or processions. These bulls look totally docile, draped with fancy blankets with their horns wreathed in flowers. They're usually led by a man holding a leash or rope, so the actual bulls were probably pretty tame. This is similar to the Apis and Mnevis bulls in ancient Egypt, which were raised to be tame and took part in religious ceremonies and processions.

As cultures clashed and societies broke down during and after the Bronze Age collapse, some details about different deities became garbled. Among other bits of confusion, Dionysus and Tauros ended up being confused with each other, to the point that the Greeks occasionally depicted Dionysus with bull horns. We don't know whether this entanglement was purposeful or accidental, but it ended up with Zagreus being associated with Dionysus rather than Tauros and the Minotaur, particularly in the Orphic Mysteries. But Orphism was a much later creation that was its own thing, separate from the far earlier Minoan religion. So in MMP, we consider Zagreus to be an aspect of our bull-god, whose other faces are Tauros Asterion and the Minotaur.

Like all other shamanic gods, Zagreus has access to the Underworld, though he's not usually depicted as a guardian of the Ancestors or the souls of the dead. However, he is a psychopomp and a conduit for communication with the dead. It's interesting that his epithet Zagreus was at one time considered to be another name for Hades, the god who ruled the Underworld. Since he is an aspect of our bull-god who is Ariadne's brother, that association makes sense, given Ariadne's status as the Queen of the Dead.

We associate Zagreus specifically with the Spring Equinox, since he's the bull who comes wreathed in flowers in the spring. This is the time of harvest in the Mediterranean, a seasonal activity that may have involved animal sacrifice in thanks for the abundance in the fields. It's also worth noting that the era when Minoan culture came into its own, around 4000-1900 BCE, is the time when the constellation Taurus marked the sunrise on Spring Equinox.

An altar to Zagreus can include any of the kinds of bull images and symbolism that you might use for Tauros and/or the

Minotaur. Colors should include the range of brown, black, tan, and cream that you'd find in a herd of cattle. But you'll also want to include springtime imagery such as flowers, preferably fresh ones, and maybe some ribbons in springtime colors as well.

Zagreus enjoys offerings of fresh flowers and floral-scented incense. He seems to prefer white wine to red, if you'd like to offer him a libation. He also likes grain, preferably in the form of wheat berries or barley groats, the crops that are harvested in the spring in the Mediterranean and that are used to feed the cattle and keep them healthy and strong.

As with Tauros, you can use stones to do divination with Zagreus' aid. You can also toss handfuls of grain and read the images they produce. And if you happen to have access to some small spring flowers like violets, a handful of them tossed onto a smooth surface can also make a good divination tool to use with Zagreus.

If you're going to embody Zagreus in ritual, a simple, rustic outfit is probably best: think "old-fashioned cowherd on his way to becoming bovine himself." You don't need to have a bull mask (we usually reserve that for embodying the Minotaur) but you do want to stick with colors that evoke cattle: browns and tans, mostly. But since this is Zagreus, a necklace or crown of fresh flowers would also be an appropriate accessory.

The Melissae

Pronunciation: MAY-lih-say, MAY-lih-sye
Epithets: *The Golden Ones, the Buzzing Ones*

The Melissae were bee-goddesses in ancient Crete. The name comes from the Greek words for honey (meli) and honeybee (melissa), words that don't have an agreed-on etymology and that may come from the Minoan language. The priestesses who served these goddesses were also called Melissae, and this is where we get the girl's name from that's still popular today. Greek myth says that Melissa was the sister of the goddess Amalthea. She was also one of the goddesses who took care of the infant Zeus (the name the Greeks gave to the Minoan Dionysus). But where

Amalthea fed him milk, Melissa fed him honey. So Minoan Crete was the land of milk and honey!

Like the Horned Ones, the Melissae are probably extremely old, dating back before Minoan culture was really built up on Crete, because they have animal rather than human forms. The Greek legends call Melissa a nymph, but this is a downgrading of her original goddess status, something we find all too often when one culture overtakes another.

The Melissae are associated with the harvest, since that's the time of year when the Minoans especially honored the ancestors (and in the Mediterranean, that time of year is the spring). Like many other Bronze Age cultures, the people of ancient Crete considered that each year's crop was blessed by the ancestors. After all, the ancestors live in the Underworld, and it looks like all those plants are growing upward from there, doesn't it? We think that at harvest time, the Minoans made offerings to the ancestors at the tombs and cemeteries on their island, when they also honored the Melissae, the goddesses who care for the ancestors in their Underworld abode.

In ancient Crete, one of the symbols for the soul was the bee. The Melissae guarded the souls of the dead in the Underworld until they could be reborn. There's also a connection between the Melissae and the shamanic practices that include journeying to the Underworld. In many cases, when they're entering the altered state of consciousness necessary for the journey, spiritworkers will hear a buzzing noise that sounds like a busy beehive. Maybe the Minoans thought they were hearing the Melissae themselves, who were guiding them to the land of the Ancestors.

The Melissae have a special relationship with Ariadne, who is the Queen Bee when she takes her place in the Underworld as a psychopomp and guardian of the dead. The Melissae may also have been associated with Eileithyia, the Minoan midwife-goddess, as well (see her section below). According to the Greek author and philosopher Porphyry, Melissa was one of the names of the goddess who took suffering away from women who were in labor. The connection is an easy one to make, since the midwife (divine or human) brings a new soul into the world. That soul comes from the land of the ancestors where it's tended by the Melissae until it's time to be reborn. So while Eileithyia delivers the baby, the Melissae deliver its soul.

At a time when sweet foods were far rarer than they are now, the ancients prized golden, delicious honey. Like most of their neighbors, the Minoans used it as a sweetener, in cooking, and in beverages. They also brewed mead, a drink similar to wine but made from fermented honey instead of grapes. They probably used mead as a gently mind-altering substance in their rituals. Some types of wild honey can be mildly hallucinogenic, depending on which plants the bees take the nectar from. And of course, the alcoholic content would also have enhanced the ritual experience.

To honor the Melissae in your ritual space you might choose shades of yellow and gold, the colors of honey and honeycomb. You can also include images of honeybees (which are native to Europe but not the Americas, interestingly enough) and honeycomb. Beeswax candles can add to the ambiance, and there are lovely candles shaped like beehives as well. Of course, the Minoans didn't have candles—they used oil lamps—but I'm pretty sure the gods understand that the world changes over time, and the Melissae do seem to enjoy beeswax candles. In addition to the other items, a small bowl of honey on your altar can serve as a reminder of the sweetness of life and the gentle care of the Melissae for the souls of the dead.

The most obvious offering for the Melissae is honey. Make sure it's the real thing, unadulterated and pure. Read labels carefully, or if you can, buy from a local beekeeper. The Melissae are also happy to accept offerings of poppyseed and fresh yellow flowers, especially wild ones. I've found them to be especially fond of dandelions.

It's difficult to do any kind of conventional divination with the Melissae. If you'd like them to help you figure something out, your best bet is to find a bunch of bees then sit down, watch, and listen. You could hang out near a beehive or find a patch of flowers where a lot of bees are doing their thing. For the best results, make an offering on your home altar first, then go in search of bees. The important part of this activity is the listening. Do it with your ears, sure, but also with your mind and especially your heart.

If you're going to embody the Melissae in ritual, aim for the honeybee colors of yellow/gold with maybe some black accents (though if you look closely at a honeybee, you'll see that they're actually just shades of yellow and tan, no black included). Any kind of flowing garment that gives the vague impression of wings or movement will work: skirt, dress, robe, cape. Please don't wear deely-bobber antennae or a Halloween bee costume; that would be disrespectful. Think, instead, of what a bee-priest or priestess might have worn in ancient Crete. Jewelry should be gold rather than silver, and accessories should be shades of yellow and gold.

Minos

Pronunciation: MEE-nos, MYE-nos
Epithets: Judge of the Dead

Here's a tricky fellow, an ancient Minoan god who was demoted to a mortal king by the Greeks. They didn't exactly portray him in a positive light, either. According to the Greek myth involving Theseus, King Minos was the king of Crete (or Knossos, depending on which version of the story you read). More important, he was the one who ordered the sacrifice of seven youths and seven maidens from Athens each year, to be fed to the Minotaur. Since the tale of Theseus and the Minotaur was the main source of information about ancient Crete during Victorian times, Sir Arthur Evans took King Minos' name as his inspiration and called the whole civilization of ancient Crete 'Minoan.' But the thing is, Minos wasn't a king. He's a god.

No one is quite sure what Minos' name means. It may be related to the Moon (more on his Moon connections below) or to other mythical founder god-kings like the Egyptian Menes. We know it's a very old name, possibly the one the Minoans used for him, because it's recorded as early as Homer's works *The Iliad* and

The Odyssey. These epic poems were written down in the 8th or 9th century BCE, but they probably include mythology and folklore from Mycenaean times several centuries earlier.

It's possible the Greeks called Minos a king because the title 'Minos' was used by the Minoan priests who represented the god during ritual. The Minoan towns appear to have been independently ruled by councils of priests and priestesses based at the temple complexes. But the Greeks, who had a hierarchical society rather than a cooperative one, may have interpreted a High Priest as a chieftain or king of the town because that's the way their own culture worked.

There are two main aspects of Minos' story that are consistent throughout all the versions, so they probably go back to his original Minoan form. The first is that he periodically died and descended to the Underworld. The second is that he was a lawgiver and a judge. These two features of Minos' tale are interconnected, since it's during his dead-in-the-Underworld time that Minos receives the laws he takes back to Crete when he returns from the Underworld. So who does he get the laws from and what are they used for? The myths give us a clue.

The standard version of the story has Minos ruling for nine years before returning to Rhea's cave, which is a symbol for the Underworld or perhaps a doorway to it. Some accounts even specify that Minos goes to the sacred cave on Mt. Ida. Now, who's in Rhea's cave who could give him a set of laws? Two deities are intimately connected with Rhea's cave: Rhea herself and her son Dionysus. Some versions of the story simply say Minos returns to Rhea's cave and receives the laws, leaving us to assume he gets them from the goddess herself. Other versions specify that he receives the laws from Cretan Zeus, that is, Dionysus. Either way, he receives his set of laws from a deity who has power in the Underworld as well as in the world above. So what does he use these laws for?

The Greek legends insist that Minos' laws were the ones on which Hellenic Greek government was based. But considering how much the values of Minoan and Greek culture differed, I find that hard to believe. The Greeks probably added that bit to give their own society the gloss of age. Other versions of the myth say that Minos used these laws to judge the souls of the dead in the Underworld. I suspect this is closer to the original version of the tale. A judge of the dead in the Underworld is a common 'job' for deities throughout the ancient world, so this isn't surprising. But what else can we figure out about Minos? There's a clue in the length of time he rules in the Upperworld in each cycle: nine years.

Specifically, the legends say Minos returned to the Underworld *every ninth year*. This wording is a clue that what we're looking at is something called *inclusive counting*. This was a common activity in the ancient world, but one that's probably unfamiliar to most people today. The reason it's unfamiliar is that we begin our counting with zero, a concept most ancient cultures didn't have. So saying Minos did something *in the ninth year* means he did it after eight years were up. In other words, his death-and-rebirth cycle is eight years long. And that brings us back to the Moon.

The Minoans were accomplished astronomers, and one of the fascinating facts they figured out is how the different celestial cycles match up. There's an eight-year-long cycle that they used as the basis of one of their calendars (they probably had several different calendar cycles based on different celestial objects). We know this from the number of marker spots on the kernoi, the stone calendar-counting devices found in the Minoan temple complexes. This cycle is eight solar years long, but also 99 lunations (Moon cycles) and five Venus cycles. They all match up in a practically magical way. After eight solar years—at the beginning of the ninth year—this cycle begins again. So Minos' activities, his death and descent to the Underworld, are linked with the Minoan sacred calendar. But what tells us that he's linked with the Moon and not the Sun or Venus?

The first clue is his genealogy. The Greeks said he was the son of Cretan Zeus (Dionysus) and Europa, the Moon-Cow goddess. In some versions of the tale, he's married to Pasiphaë, another face of the sacred Moon-Cow. So is Minos yet another Moon deity, along with the male Horned Ones? How many Moon gods did the Minoans have? Isn't this getting a little ridiculous?

It's true, the Horned Ones we've already met were gods and goddesses of the Moon. They're probably the oldest Minoan Moon deities, descended from Neolithic-era totemic animal spirits. To add to the confusion, there's also the possibility that Europa and Pasiphaë were Sun goddesses before their iconography shifted to the Moon. But we have to remember that Minoan religion, like Egyptian religion, was multi-layered. When the Minoans encountered or developed new deities and myths, they simply added them onto what they already had. This is how gods like Dionysus ended up with so many different faces and functions and how the Minoan pantheon can sport so many Moon deities.

Minos behaves like many of the Mesopotamian and Levantine Moon gods such as Nanna and Sin and the Phrygian moon-god Mên. We don't know whether he was borrowed into the Minoan pantheon from some other region or was simply influenced by these other cultures that the Minoans traded with. One major characteristic of all these Moon gods is their wisdom, which is displayed in Minos' lawgiving and judgment.

If we want to talk about Moon symbolism, we should look at those ill-fated Athenian kids from the Greek story of Theseus— seven girls and seven boys shipped off to be Minotaur chow every year. The number 14 in the ancient world was consistently linked with the Moon because 14 is the number of days in half a Moon cycle (from full to new or from new to full). So that's another pointer toward Minos' Moon connection.

One other interesting bit about Minos is that he may have been a triple god; that fits in with the other triplicities in the pantheon. Throughout the different versions of his story, he's described as one of three brothers. Now, Minos is always the 'highest' of the three—the most successful, the superior one, and so on. But there are always three. The names change a bit from one account to another, but the two most common names for Minos' brothers are

Rhadamanthys and Sarpedon. They're all described as judges in the Underworld.

This triplicity suggests the possibility that the Minoans thought of the Moon as having three phases. This was common in the ancient world. The waxing, full, and waning Moon were viewed as three separate parts of the cycle. The new (dark) Moon was viewed as a 'null' time, or a lack of the Moon, before the cycle began again. Many ancient cultures watched for the first sliver of crescent Moon in the sky after the new Moon and counted that as the first day of the lunation. That's a much easier defining point than either the full Moon or the new Moon, each of which appears, to the naked eye, to last for three days.

If you'd like to include Minos in your sacred space, you have several different options to choose from. You could focus on him as a god in the form of a man. The Greeks tended to portray him as an older man, bearded and wearing a crown or diadem, sitting on his seat of judgment. So artwork or figurines with that kind of image would work here, if that appeals to you. We really don't know how the Minoans saw him, though there are plenty of Minoan seals that show bearded older men (possibly priests, possibly gods) wearing long robes.

Underworld imagery would also work, like red foods or photographs and artwork of caves. And of course, you could include the Moon in any of its forms: slim crescent, quarter moon, full, or anywhere in between. The one symbol that Minos doesn't appear to be associated with is horns, so if you're going for Moon symbolism with him, stick with the actual Moon and not the sacred horns or similar images. The colors you choose for your altar should evoke the Underworld: grey and black for the most part, with some white and cream. The Underworld isn't necessarily a bad place, but it can be stark and colorless from the human point of view.

Minos enjoys offerings of pure, fresh water, preferably from a natural source. Bottled spring water works just fine here in case you don't have access to a lake or river. To make your offering extra special, pour the water into a bowl and leave it out in the light of the full Moon before putting it on the altar. Minos is the only Minoan deity I've encountered who doesn't seem to care whether you pour a libation or simply set an already-filled container of liquid on the altar. The others clearly prefer to have the libation poured into a container on the altar or on the ground nearby. Minos does have one preference, though: if you can, choose a black bowl to put the water in. And, in stark contrast to the rest of our pantheon, he really doesn't care for wine.

Minos is practically divination incarnate, or at least, in the form of a deity. He's very easy to work with as a guide when you're doing divination, but be aware that he doesn't sugar-coat his messages. To do divination with his assistance, choose a pendulum with a dark stone or scry in water (not wine) in a dark bowl.

Minos is an older, authoritative figure from ancient mythology, so aim for that vibe if you're embodying him. You don't have to have a beard, but it helps. You can go for any kind of outfit that evokes the ancient world: a regular or diagonally-wrapped robe like we see men wearing on the Minoan seals, or even a Greek or Roman-style garment. Your clothing should, by preference, be long rather than short, and you should maintain a stately bearing during the ritual.

Eileithyia

Pronunciation: ay-LAY-thee-ah or ee-LEE-thee-ah
Epithets: The Deliverer

Eileithyia is the midwife-goddess, the deity who protects pregnant women and safeguards them during labor and childbirth, but there's more to her than that. Her name isn't Greek, so when we call to Eileithyia, we're probably using a form that's very close to her original Minoan name.

Her cult in ancient Crete was so popular that she had her own cave just south of Amnisos, the port city on the coast of Crete just north of Knossos. Eileithyia's cave was first used in Neolithic times, somewhere between 7000 and 5000 BCE, and continued to be a goal of sacred pilgrimage until about 400 BCE, long after Minoan civilization was gone.

Tradition says that Eileithyia herself was born in this cave, which is why it's sacred to her. The cave includes an altar built by the Minoans in a spot surrounded by large, pillar-shaped stalagmites. The stalagmites create a natural focal point and they include one special pair that are called Mother and Child (one is taller than the other). Outside the cave there was a paved plaza in Minoan times. Near the cave entrance there were several buildings that probably served both Eileithyia's clergy and the pilgrims who journeyed to the cave.

It makes sense that a goddess of childbirth would have one of the longest-running cult centers on Crete, since every generation has children. And of course, pregnancy and childbirth in the ancient world were a good bit more dangerous than they are now, even with the best midwifery of the time and in a clean place like one of the Minoan cities. You can bet that a lot of pregnant women made the pilgrimage to her cave, just for a little extra luck.

As the bringer of new humans into the world to begin their life's journey, Eileithyia is associated with the later Greek Fates as well as the earlier Minoan Melissae. This makes sense in terms of bringing the new soul from the Underworld and the ancestors. The woman births the baby's body, but Eileithyia helps and also delivers its soul into this world. Like the Melissae, Eileithyia was given offerings of honey in ancient times.

She's also connected with the Eleusinian Mysteries, which appear to have begun on Crete and later moved to the Greek mainland. The name of the Greek town where the Mysteries were held—Eleusis—isn't Greek. Instead, it appears to be associated with both Elysium (the Greek abode of the ancestors) and Eileithyia's name.

In Greek art Eileithyia is often shown carrying a torch, an item the Greeks said stood for the burning pain of childbirth. I'd like to suggest an alternate interpretation. If the torch is one of her earlier symbols from a time in Minoan civilization when women were more honored and cherished, then it might be a symbol of comfort for the laboring mother. It might also represent the passage of the baby from the darkness of the womb to the light of the world.

We think Eileithyia's torch had another meaning as well. In MMP, we consider her to be Ariadne's torch-bearer during the "dead" season that Ariadne spends in the Underworld. In a sense, this makes Eileithyia the Dark Sun or Underworld Sun goddess, similar to Hekate from the Greek mainland. Some of us view her as a death-midwife as well as a birth-midwife. Both of these are liminal, transition times that can be dangerous, times when the soul moves from one realm to another.

Eileithyia also has a connection with Dionysus through the sacred silver fir tree that's one of his symbols. The resin of the silver fir—the sacred substance that was added to wine in Dionysian rites—was called the 'menses of Eileithyia,' in other words, her menstrual blood. It's possible the resin had a medicinal use during childbirth. And the tree itself offers a connection as well. Sacred birthing trees were common in Crete and throughout the Bronze Age world. They were considered to be the locations of the birth of various gods, Dionysus included. And of course, even a goddess needs a midwife, so who better to help than a divine one?

If you'd like to include Eileithyia in your sacred space, I recommend that you set up a separate altar or shrine for her, since she has a specific job, if you see what I mean. I've found that she's helpful not just for human pregnancy and birth but also for the birth of new projects and new phases of life. She can also help you put yourself back together and be symbolically reborn after difficult times, and she does an amazing job of helping those of us who are jaded and worn by the worries of the grown-up world to find our childhood innocence again.

Some possible symbols that can help you focus on Eileithyia include figurines and artwork of pregnant women or mothers with babies. Obviously, those focus on her role as the helper of women in pregnancy and childbirth. But she has plenty of other symbols you can use if you want to concentrate on her ability to help you with a fresh start of any kind. Fresh pine/fir greenery and pine/fir incense and essential oils are good choices. I really like the imagery of the torch lighting the way, illuminating a new path. You're not likely to be able to hang a torch on the wall of a modern home, but images of torches will work. You could also use a smaller version of a torch-like flame, maybe one of the wood-wick candles that are so popular now. These have a thin piece of wood rather than a string for a wick, and they crackle when they burn, just like a torch or a wood fire does.

Eileithyia can also be a supportive presence during the time a loved one is moving toward death. If you'd like her help under such circumstances, I recommend setting up an altar just for that purpose, even if you already have an altar that honors her. Include on the altar not just symbols for Eileithyia, but photos and mementos of the person who is passing. If you can, keep a candle (a tiny torch substitute) lit on the altar at all times, or someplace safe nearby, like in a fireplace.

The ancients gave Eileithyia offerings of the delicious things in life: honey, sweets made with honey, grapes, and pomegranates. You could include these as a reminder of the sweetness of every kind of birth and rebirth. We've found that she also enjoys poppyseeds, milk, mead and fresh-baked bread. Gold, white, and green—the colors of honey, torchlight, and the sacred fir—can evoke her in your sacred space in the form of altar cloths, candles, candleholders, bowls, cups, and any other accessories you'd like to include.

Divination with Eileithyia is best done by scrying in a dark room, lit only by candlelight. You can scry in a black mirror (obsidian or black-painted glass) or in water that's in a black bowl. She's mostly interested in matters of transition from one life state to another, so those are the best subjects to address in divination with her help.

If you'll be embodying Eileithyia in ritual, choose clothing in her trio of colors: gold, white, and green, with an emphasis on the gold and white. She's a goddess of liminal times, so you can be veiled to embody her if you like, but it's not required. Accessories and jewelry should be simple and practical, as befits a working midwife. If you have long hair, you can wrap it up in a scarf like the figures in the Mature Women fresco from Xeste 3, who we think might be midwives.

Daedalus

Pronunciation: DEH-duh-lus or DEE-duh-lus
Epithets: Talos, The Craftsman

You may have heard of the legendary architect and craftsman Daedalus via the story of his building of the labyrinth to hide the monstrous Minotaur, or his escape from Crete with his son Icarus via two pairs of hand-crafted wings. These stories come from the Roman writer Ovid, who lived nearly 1500 years after the destruction of the Minoan cities. And like much of Minoan mythology that was recorded in later times, these stories were put together from garbled fragments that somehow managed to survive the destruction of the Minoan cities and the Bronze Age collapse. So obviously, take them with a big pinch of salt.

In MMP, we consider Daedalus to be a smith and inventor god, a face of our Young God Korydallos. Daedalus is the skilled craftsman who took the gifts that the Mothers gave humanity and taught people how to use them to make beautiful and useful things. Bear in mind, the Minoans were a Bronze Age culture, so metal smithing didn't look the way you probably think of it. When someone mentions smithing, most people think of a forge with a huge anvil where the smith hammers the red-hot metal into shape. But bronze smithing doesn't work that way.

Bronze smithing does involve fire, both to purify the ore into usable metal and then to melt the metal. The remains of bellows have been found at Minoan sites where there were forges. But in bronze smithing, the metals (copper and tin) are melted together and then poured into a carved stone mold. Once the metal has cooled off, the item—a dagger blade, for instance, or a figurine— can be removed from the mold and finished by grinding a sharp edge onto the blade or smoothing down the shape of the figurine.

In *The Iliad*, Homer says that Daedalus built Ariadne's dancing floor. It's thought that the circular folk dances of Crete originated at harvest festivals where dancing took place on the outdoor threshing floors. This may be how Daedalus came to be associated with the labyrinth, which later people thought was a complex building, but which may originally have been a design marked on floors for rituals, or even a type of spiraling dance.

Another name we associate with Daedalus is Talos, the mythical bronze automaton that guarded the shores of ancient Crete. In MMP we consider him not as a mechanical man, but a god whose mother gave the gift of bronze-smithing to her people. In that sense, we can think of Talos/Daedalus (and Korydallos) as an embodiment of that gift. Talos' connection with the Sun in classical-era mythology points us back to Korydallos and his mother, Therasia. Apparently the word talôs can mean "the Sun" in the Cretan dialect of Greek, so there's another connection. The Greek mythographer Pseudo-Apollodorus said that Talos was the last of the "bronze generation" and was a "bronze man." Maybe he wasn't an actual man made of bronze, but rather, a patron deity of bronze-smithing in the era when that skill died out, to be replaced by iron-working.

Regardless, Daedalus has his full place in our pantheon as the patron deity of craftspeople and inventors. If you're looking for inspiration for a hands-on project, he's a good choice to turn to. And if you'd like to devote a significant portion of your life to some kind of handcraft or artisanal skill, I recommend developing a long-term relationship with him.

Though Daedalus is traditionally associated with metal smithing and inventing nifty gadgets like wings that will actually make people fly, we've found that he's also a very helpful deity for anyone who practices traditional handcraft skills, either as a hobby or professionally. So think along the lines of bookbinding, wood carving, jewelry making, that sort of thing. There are some activities he's not so good at, though, that appear to be the purview of other deities instead. Pottery, for instance, is considered to be Rhea's provenance. And the fiber arts (spinning, weaving, sewing, and so on) are Arachne's thing.

An altar to Daedalus won't necessarily look like altars to other deities. Instead of figurines and candles, it might hold items you've made: mechanical gadgets, wood you've whittled into shape, some of the tools you use in those pursuits. He and the closely related Daktyls and Hekaterides (listed below) are the only Minoan deities I've encountered who really prefer oil lamps to candles. The others don't seem to have a preference, but Daedalus and the Daktyls and Hekaterides really like oil lamps. Altars to him also seem to work better without a lot of drapery like altar cloths. A bare wooden tabletop is more suited to his style.

In terms of offerings, lighting an oil lamp to him is a good, basic offering. If you'd like his help with a handcrafting pursuit, make an item and dedicate it to him as an offering, leaving it permanently on the altar. He's not too keen on wine or food as offerings, though interestingly, he will accept libations of olive oil and castor oil.

Daedalus has a narrow range of ways in which he can help with divination. Don't come to him for clarification about life's deep problems. But if you can't figure out how to get your latest invention to work, or if you're trying to figure out which skill to learn next, he can probably help you. The pendulum is his preferred divination method, preferably with a metal weight, ideally one made of bronze or brass. He doesn't much like iron or steel.

If you're embodying Daedalus in ritual, think of a brilliant ancient-world inventor and mad scientist as you decide how to dress. A simple tunic would work just fine, or even later Greek or Roman-style clothing. Depending on the content of the ritual, it might be appropriate to carry some sort of tool: a wood-carving knife, for instance, or a chisel. Though it's all right to use iron or steel tools in this situation if you don't have access to bronze ones, avoid using anything obviously modern like a screwdriver or an adjustable wrench.

The Daktyls and the Hekaterides

Pronunciation: DAK-tills and heh-kah-TEH-ree-days
Epithets: Hands of Great Skill

These ten demigods and demigoddesses are associated with two particular skills: bronze smithing and pottery making. They are Rhea's children—sort of. At least, they're her creations. When she was in her sacred cave at Midwinter, laboring to birth the Divine Child, she dug her fingers into the Earth, gripping and grounding herself, giving herself the strength to bring her baby into the world. And as the baby was born, from her finger-marks rose up the five Daktyls and the five Hekaterides: Hands of Great Skill.

In MMP we associate the Daktyls with metal smithing, particularly bronze, and we associate the Hekaterides with pottery making. We consider the Daktyls to be demi-gods and the Hekaterides to be demi-goddesses, each set of five presiding over their particular artisanal skill. We've considered the possibility that these two occupations—bronze smithing and pottery making—were gendered in Crete, with men being smiths and women being potters, given the genders of the patron deities. There's really no way to tell whether or not that was the case, and in modern terms, the Daktyls and Hekaterides will happily support anyone who is practicing their craft, regardless of gender.

An altar to the Daktyls or the Hekaterides (depending on your preferred craft) is best set up in the area where you're doing the pottery or metal smithing. Like Daedalus, they seem to prefer a bare wooden tabletop rather than an altar cloth, and oil lamps rather than candles. Include representations of your craft on the altar, maybe small items you've made and bits of your raw materials. Since the symbolism of hands is important here, you could also include your handprint in some way, maybe pressed in paint on paper or impressed into clay.

Lighting an oil lamp is the most basic offering to the Daktyls and/or Hekaterides. They also appreciate offerings of small pieces of your raw materials (metal ore or clay). The best offering you can give them is your work: dedicate a project to them, think about them as you're making it, and thank them publicly when it's done.

The Daktyls and Hekaterides aren't particularly helpful in terms of general divination, but if you're trying to figure out what to do for your next project, they can probably help you. They're also a good resource for those times when you're working on a project and can't get it to do what you want or are frustrated that you're not learning the skill the way you expected. If you want to ask the Daktyls and/or the Hekaterides to help with a situation like I've described, use your favorite method to reach a meditative state, put your hands on the altar, and present them with your problem or frustration. Then listen carefully for the answer.

The Daktyls and Hekaterides should only be embodied in ritual in groups of five, never alone. Your dress should reflect the crafts that these deities represent: bronze and other metallic colors for the Daktyls (bronze smithing) and warm earth tones for the Hekaterides (the clay of pottery). Garments should be simple and timeless so people can focus more on the color and motion than the style.

Ourania

Pronunciation: oh-RAH-nee-ah
Epithets: Great Cosmic Mother, Mother of Darkness and Stars
We come full circle by ending the pantheon list as we began, with a mother goddess. In MMP we consider Ourania to be one of the mother goddesses, but she's a bit further removed from us than the Three Mothers, whose realms are land, sky, and sea. In a sense, she's the greatest of the mother goddesses, the Great Cosmic Mother.

Ourania is the name the later Greeks gave to an earlier goddess, but of course they demoted her a few notches, turning her into the muse of astronomy. Her Greek name gives us a clue to her original function: she's the cosmos, the starry sky, the very fabric of the universe. If you're into quantum physics, you can envision her as the quantum foam, the not-quite-material substance out of which everything is made. She has another name as well, an earlier Mycenaean Greek name from the Linear B tablets: Diwia. This comes from the Greek word root for deity, the same root that eventually gives us the name Zeus. In other words, this is a name that simply means Goddess, the Highest One.

Astronomy—the study of the starry skies—was a central focus of Minoan sacred life, at least for the clergy. The ordinary people probably didn't know much more than the basics about the Sun and the Moon. But the staff in the temple complexes kept track of complicated calendars based on the cycles of the Moon, the Sun, Venus, and several different stars. They must have spent many nights on the temple rooftops, watching the stars wheel through the sky, rising and setting over the tops of the sacred mountain peaks. To them, the entire process was holy. Ourania's motions drive the cosmos, turning the wheels of time. She's the musician who plays the music of the spheres, and she is also the spheres themselves. Some people like to think of her as a force of nature, a cosmic power, rather than an anthropomorphic goddess.

The idea of a cosmic goddess is probably a little harder to visualize than, say, an Earth goddess. Some of us experience Ourania as a black vulture, her wings spread out across the depths of space. Perhaps that's her we see on the pillars at Gobekli Tepe, a temple from the region and era that the Minoans' ancestors came from. Some of us also experience Ourania as a cosmic cow goddess, with the spots on her hide as the stars that are spread out across the sky. Perhaps, eons ago, it was her milk that spurted to make the Milky Way. Though we consider Ourania to be a mother goddess, most of us find it difficult to envision her in human form unless she's simply a veiled figure, mysterious and shadowy.

One of my favorite ways to focus on Ourania is to take a bowl of water outdoors at night and look at the reflections of the stars on the surface of the water. This works best with a bowl that's a solid, dark color on the inside, preferably black, but dark green, purple, or blue will also work. Catching starlight in water is an ancient kind of magic. When you feel like the water's full of starlight, you can bring it back inside and leave it on your altar as a charged object, full of Ourania's energy.

There are plenty of ways to incorporate Ourania into your sacred space, though it's not really necessary to set up an altar to her. She exists everywhere, all the time, so simply focusing on her from time to time is often enough. But if you want to devote an altar to her, any kind of celestial-themed items can provide a cosmic focus. There are lots of different kinds of celestial-print fabrics that would make great altar cloths. There's also a lot of beautiful space photography available these days, thanks to NASA and the other space agencies, and those kinds of images certainly evoke the cosmos. Though it's not at all Minoan, I like Renaissance-era artwork that shows the celestial objects—Sun, Moon, planets, stars—because it feels less modern than photography, so it draws me mentally toward the past. Star-shaped candle holders are fairly easy to come by, too. And there's a range of colors you can use, depending on which ones make you think of the cosmos: deep blue to black, the shiny white of twinkling stars, metallic gold and silver.

Ourania likes offerings made outside at night, beneath the light of the stars. Her preferred offering is pure water from a natural source. It's best to set the water out in the starlight for a short time before offering it. Then, when you're ready, pour the offering out into a dark-colored bowl. If you have a bowl made of stone, that's preferable, or you could set a black or dark green stone in a bowl made of another material before pouring the water into it. Leave the water out until sunrise, then dispose of it by pouring it onto the ground.

Since she is at once everywhere and nowhere, Ourania isn't always much of a help with divination. Her responses to human questions can be vague and confusing, or oddly specific in ways that can be difficult to interpret. Still, if you're feeling adventurous and would like to give it a try, scrying in a dark bowl of water, preferably beneath a starry sky, is your best bet.

Because of Ourania's unique status as a cosmic goddess, if you'll be embodying her in ritual, your face must be covered.

Though we refer to her as a mother goddess, she's not nearly as easy to anthropomorphize as the others. We consider it respectful not to put a human face on her image. Choose shades of black, grey, and white, either plain or with cosmic or celestial patterns. Your entire head should be veiled and you should present as more of a shadowy figure than a human being.

Chapter 4:
The Minoan Sacred Calendar

The eight-fold wheel of the year that's so popular in Neopaganism is a modern invention, a compilation of several different seasonal and celestial cycles into one neat-and-tidy circle. It works, of course, is used by many different groups and traditions, and is internally consistent. But it definitely doesn't go back as far as ancient Crete. We've developed our MMP sacred calendar from a combination of archaeology, dance ethnography, archaeoastronomy and comparative mythology with a healthy dose of "try it and see if it works" thrown in.

As far as we can tell, the Minoans didn't have a balanced yearly calendar like the eightfold Wheel of the Year. Their sacred festivals grew out of their lives as sailors and farmers on and around an island in the Mediterranean Sea. The opening of sailing season was a kind of new year celebration, the beginning of the time when many Minoans boarded ships and left to trade in distant lands. And because the summer is the 'dead time' in the Mediterranean, the beginning of the rainy season in the autumn was another kind of new year celebration in ancient Crete. That's the time of year when the agricultural cycle starts again, when the farmers plow the fields and plant their seeds. This is similar to the way the northern European new year was celebrated at the Spring Equinox for many centuries, since springtime is the beginning of the agricultural cycle there. The lives of the sailors and the farmers of ancient Crete intertwined, creating a vibrant, rhythmic cycle every year that took into account both the land and the sea.

A series of MMP sacred festivals clusters around the agricultural new year in the autumn. In ancient times, these festivals may have made up a holiday season that lasted the better part of a month. This is similar to the way we have a multi-week-long winter holiday season in the modern western world. Our autumnal MMP holiday season begins with the Feast of Grapes, a Dionysian celebration of the grape harvest. It continues with the Minoan precursor to the Eleusinian Mysteries, which took place over a period of ten days. This 'holiday season' portion of the Minoan sacred year ends up with the new year's celebrations at the Autumn Equinox.

In addition to the autumn holiday season, the Minoans celebrated the Winter and Summer Solstices, a harvest festival around the time of the Spring Equinox, and other sacred days. It's possible that their sacred calendar was as full as the ancient Roman one. There's still a lot we don't know about what they celebrated, and when.

As I mentioned before, the planting and harvesting times in the Mediterranean are backwards from the northern temperate zone. If you feel comfortable celebrating these days based on the Mediterranean seasons, by all means do so, but it's perfectly fine to reverse them (with the agricultural new year in the spring and harvest in the autumn) if that fits your local climate. A big part of practicing an Earth-oriented spirituality is honoring the Earth wherever you are. I'm sure the Minoans would understand.

The festivals that make up the Minoan sacred calendar were group events, but these days it can be difficult to find other Pagans to celebrate with. Fortunately for us, it's possible to observe these sacred times as a solitary as well. Instead of a complicated ritual, try using the devotionals to the deities who are the focus of each festival. You could decorate your sacred space appropriately for the occasion and meditate on the mythology, the legends and tales that go with each time of the year. You can also use the standard ritual format in Chapter 5 to perform your own ceremony at any time of the year.

The Festivals

The Blessing of the Ships

Third Monday in May. The Minoans were a seagoing people: they fished, they traded, and they traveled in boats and ships. So it makes sense that they would have incorporated these major facets of their lives into their spiritual practice. The Blessing of the Ships marks what would have been the beginning of the sailing season in ancient Crete, and in that sense it's a sort of new year celebration.

We don't know for certain what the Minoans did to bless their ships, crews, and cargo before a voyage, but it's a good bet they did something. Bits of information that made it through the Bronze Age collapse and ended up in the works of later writers, combined with archaeoastronomy research, suggest that the Minoan sailing season had a definite beginning and ending: the heliacal rising of the Pleiades in mid-May and the heliacal setting of that constellation in late October to early November. This makes sense, given that the winds during the wintertime would have made sailing in that era pretty hazardous.

So what on earth does *heliacal rising* mean? Some stars, like the ones in the constellation Ursa Major (also known as the Big Dipper or the Plough) are visible all year long in the northern hemisphere. They never dip below the horizon. But other stars appear and disappear at various times of the year. For instance, if you live in the northern hemisphere, you can only see the constellation Orion in the wintertime.

The heliacal rising of one of these disappearing-and-reappearing stars happens when the star has been invisible for a while. Then one morning it will shine for a few moments just above the eastern horizon, right before the Sun rises (the word *heliacal* means having to do with the Sun, who was called Helios by the Greeks). After that, it will come into view for a little bit longer each day, but that first appearance is the magical moment of its heliacal rising. The heliacal rising of a star was considered a sign of good fortune in the ancient world, and it still is by modern astrologers. Many ancient cultures kept records of the heliacal risings of different stars. The Egyptians, for instance, based their yearly calendar on the heliacal rising of Sirius.

The term heliacal setting is, obviously, related to heliacal rising. In fact, it's kind of its opposite. When a star has been visible for a while, like the Pleiades are in the Mediterranean during sailing season, eventually it will work its way across the sky until it's setting in the west right around sunset. The heliacal setting is the last day when the star sets after sunset and the Sun is already far enough below the western horizon that the star is visible for a few moments in the evening twilight.

Due to precession, the dates for the heliacal rising and setting of stars slowly drift over time. Over the 1500 years or so of the height of Minoan civilization, the dates drifted about two weeks, which isn't enough to significantly impact the timing of their sailing season. In early Minoan times, the heliacal rising of the Pleiades was around May 1. By the time the cities fell, it hit about mid-May. Now, in 2020, it's around Summer Solstice. So the actual heliacal rising no longer coincides with the beginning of sailing season. During Minoan times, the heliacal setting drifted from late October to early November; now it's closer to Winter Solstice.

Based on the probable beginning of sailing season in Minoan times, we've set the Blessing of the Ships on the third Monday in May. That's about when the heliacal rising of the Pleiades occurred in the late Bronze Age. And if you're able to take the day off work as a religious holiday, it gives you a three-day weekend. Like this festival's autumn counterpart, Harbor Home, our modern date for this one makes it a *floating* holiday—very appropriate for a festival that focuses on ships and sailing! You can check out more details about Harbor Home in its listing later on in this chapter.

If you have a boat (or a surfboard or a jet-ski) you can bless it for safety and enjoyment on this day. Anyone who will regularly be sailing/riding/surfing should be present so they can partake in the blessing as well. Though the name of this festival is the Blessing of the Ships, it's really a sanctification of the entire process of going out on the water, including the people and gear involved. Begin by making an offering to Posidaeja, even if you're boating on fresh water and not on the open ocean. Her preferred libation is pure water from a natural source, but you could also pour out a small offering of white wine if you like. If you're offering wine, pour it into a bowl or onto the ground, not into the water. You could also offer a small object that you value but that won't do any harm to the body of water if you throw it in. Some good options include a semiprecious stone, a small figurine, or even a few coins. If it feels like you're losing something when you toss it into the water, it will work.

Fig. 8: Ships from the Flotilla fresco, Akrotiri

Some traditions in various parts of the world involve making garlands or wreaths out of fresh flowers as an act of celebration, then giving these to the body of water as an offering. If this idea inspires you, you could include it in your offerings. Just be sure to use entirely biodegradable materials so you don't do any harm. Polyester ribbon is every bit as damaging to wildlife as fishing line is. The best option would be to make something like a daisy chain that doesn't involve materials other than just the flowers themselves.

Once you've made your offering, you can ask Posidaeja's blessing on your boat or other water-borne conveyance. The simplest method is simply to scoop up some water from the lake or ocean and pour it over the prow of the boat. You can also make herb-infused water (herb tea, essentially) from rosemary, rue, sage, or myrtle and sprinkle that to bless your boat. Be sure also to bless the people who will be sailing or boating, preferably by asperging them lightly (this is not the occasion for a water fight).

If you want to get fancy, you can decorate your boat with garlands and streamers for the occasion and wear bright, festive clothes. You could also sing sea shanties and play drums as both a celebration and an offering. If you're doing this with friends who also have boats, you could form a flotilla and have a ceremonial procession around the bay or down to the next inlet.

I've always imagined that the Minoans set seven doves loose on the docks at their Blessing of the Ships, reading divinations for the upcoming sailing season in their flight (the seven doves are symbolic of the seven stars of the Pleiades). You probably don't have seven doves handy for such an activity, but you could try casting seven stones or bones on the dock or on the ship's deck, or tossing seven feathers into the air.

Given that we're modern Pagans and that we don't all own boats or live near the water, we can also repurpose this festival as one that blesses the beginning of a journey, or even of the summer vacation season. In this case, you might be performing this ritual at a time other than the third Monday in May, and that's all right. Use the occasion to consecrate your car, your RV, your motorcycle or bicycle—whatever conveyance you'll be using to make your journey, as well as the people who will be traveling in it. If you'll be hiking, use it to bless your hiking boots and any gear you'll be taking along with you as well as yourself for the journey ahead. If you'll be traveling via common carrier (airplane, train, bus) you can perform the blessing using a printout of your ticket as a stand-in for the vehicle and its route. To do a slightly more land-focused divination for your journey, you could go with the seven feathers I mentioned above, or try tossing a handful of seeds (anything but poppyseeds—they represent the Underworld and hence, death) or even blowing a dandelion puffball. May all your journeys be safe and pleasant.

The Height of Summer

Summer Solstice, approximately 21 June. Due to the many layers of religion that built up and were added on over the course of the centuries of Minoan civilization, we have multiple layers of mythology to celebrate at the Summer Solstice. Our Midsummer celebrations involve Therasia and Dionysus as well as some other deities; you'll find these same two deities in our Winter Solstice festival as well.

If you recall, summer is the "dead time" in the Mediterranean, and it's all because of Therasia's ferocity. This is the point in the year when she reaches the height of her power, her intense heat and light beating down on the Earth during long days, with the shorts nights bringing little relief. At the Summer Solstice, we stand in awe of the Sun-Mother's power, the force that drives the life on our planet. Like the ancient Minoans, we light bonfires on hilltops and sing and dance in her honor. This is also the time to capture the sunlight in a bowl or pot of water and then drink it for healing and blessings, giving thanks to Therasia for all she has given us.

During the height of their use, there were more than two dozen peak sanctuaries across Crete, and they all show evidence of repeated bonfires. The interesting thing is, they may have formed a sort of sacred communication network across the island since almost all of them can be seen by other nearby peak sanctuaries. In other words, we can imagine that on the morning of Summer Solstice, the clergy at the farthest east peak sanctuary (Petsofas) would have been the first to see the sunrise. As soon as they saw that first burst of sunlight, they would have lit their bonfire, which would have been visible from four or five nearby peak sanctuaries. As soon as those others saw the first bonfire, they would light theirs, and so on across the island, a wave of light moving east to west with fires blazing on the mountaintops to welcome the Midsummer Sun. Around the world and across time, bonfires have long been a major part of Sun festivals in many cultures. They're particularly associated with the sunrise and sunset on Summer Solstice.

In addition to Therasia's yearly cycle, at the Summer Solstice we also focus on Dionysus. He was born at Midwinter, and now he's ready to emerge from Rhea's cave and come out into the world. This festival is his rite of passage into adulthood. It also celebrates the sacred marriage of Dionysus with Ariadne, a scene we find on a number of Minoan seals. But Ariadne and Dionysus aren't husband-and-wife consorts the way many later Greek divine couples are. Ariadne and Dionysus are independent, each one going about his or her 'job' separately throughout the year. They come together at this sacred time to unite the realms and to celebrate the fullness of the year, the height of the Sun and the power of the year-king. So maybe "marriage" isn't the best term to use, but "mating" sounds a little too much like animal breeding. Let's just say they have a sacred rendezvous.

The Throne Room in the Knossos temple complex has some interesting sunrise alignments that give us some clues as to how the myth and ritual may have played out in Minoan times. Specifically, it has sunrise alignments for the solstices. At Midwinter the rising sun shines on the 'throne,' Rhea's birthing chair (find out more in the section below about the Winter Solstice). But at Midsummer it illuminates the entrance to the adyton, the sunken portion of the floor that Sir Arthur Evans took to be a huge built-in bathtub. Similar adyta are found in many Minoan temple complexes and ritual areas, and none of them show any signs of being used with water. I believe they're symbolic, man-made caves. And the one in the Throne Room would be Rhea's cave, the refuge where she hid the newborn Dionysus and the place from which he emerges into the world at Summer Solstice. Anyone lucky enough to attend the Summer Solstice ritual at Knossos would have watched as the rising Sun edged above the nearby mountains. Moments later, a sunbeam would have sliced across the courtyard to shine a spotlight on the top step of the adyton, just in time for Dionysus to emerge in all his glory.

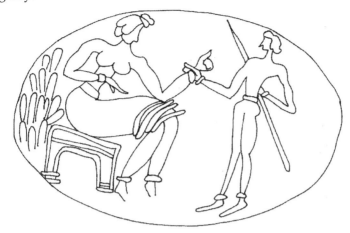

Fig. 9: Seal ring with divine pair, Mycenae

Even if they couldn't participate in the ritual in the Throne Room, the people would have enjoyed the processions and mystery plays the clergy put on for the public out on the plazas and viaducts to the west and south of the temple complex. The day would have begun when the clergy on the temple rooftops spotted the first rays of sunrise and announced it via torches and perhaps the blowing of the conch trumpets, moments before the Throne Room received its sunbeam. But the rooftop astronomers may not have been the only ones watching for that sacred sunrise.

Since Summer Solstice is the time when Dionysus becomes an adult, it may also have been a time for rites of passage into adulthood for boys (girls would have had their rites of passage whenever they began menstruating). The Kouretes, the infant Dionysus' guardians at Rhea's cave, may represent a clergy group associated with Dionysus who were demoted to a type of folkloric dancer in later Greek mythology. The name Kouretes comes from kouros, the Greek word for a youth (teenage boy), and Dionysus was called 'the greatest kouros.' The Kouretes are associated in Greek myth with coming-of-age ceremonies for young men. Since the Summer Solstice is connected with the sacred marriage of

Dionysus and Ariadne, it may also have been a time of sexual initiation for the young men who were being acknowledged as new adults. It would be appropriate to hold MMP coming-of-age rites for boys at this time. There's one in *Ariadne's Thread*, though I recommend recasting it using the standard MMP ritual format, found in Chapter 5.

As with any solar-oriented festival, Sun symbols and sunny colors would be appropriate. Therasia's sacred colors are blood-red and golden yellow, the colors of the murex and saffron dyes. Actual gold or gold-colored metal is also a good choice. Wedding-type decorations would also be fitting, especially wreaths and garlands of flowers (but skip the 'white for virginity' bit that modern weddings include—that was probably not an issue in Minoan culture, where women were independent and didn't 'belong' to men the way they did in later societies). Some of the seals from ancient Crete depict images of the sacred marriage, with the god and goddess in a ritual pose on top of a sacred mountain, so that artwork would make a good addition to your celebrations. For the coming-of-age aspect of this festival, Dionysus' colors (deep purple, deep green, and gold) would be good choices. If you'd like to include the Kouretes, their main symbols are shields and spears which are used as percussion instruments. If you don't happen to have the appropriate weaponry on hand, drums and rattles would make good substitutes. And if you decide to dance a little in time with the percussion, I'm sure Dionysus would be pleased.

This celebration occurs during the crispy-dry, brown-and-dead summer season on Crete, so it's not really a nature festival as such. The Minoans probably celebrated in the temples, local shrines, and peak sanctuaries. There may also have been 'appearances' of a priest playing the part of Dionysus emerging from the sacred caves on the island. If you live in a region that's not quite so well-broiled during the summer, you could make this an outdoor occasion and bask in the glory of the summer Sun. Or, for the more intrepid, you could get up early and watch the Sun rise, coming up over the horizon the way Dionysus appears as he rises out of the adyton or the mouth of his mother's cave.

Feast of Grapes

31 August. Just like other harvest-based festivals, the actual date of the Feast of Grapes would have varied from year to year depending on when the crop was ready to harvest. Classical sources tell us it typically occurred at a date that falls from the end of August to the beginning of September in the modern calendar.

The Feast of Grapes focuses on Dionysus, the god of wine and ecstasy. He's embodied in the grapevine and the fruit, so the harvest is his annual symbolic death. When he dies, he returns to the Underworld for a time. This gives his worshipers access to the Underworld for healing and communion with the Ancestors. The Feast of Grapes has some similarities to the northern European celebrations of the dying-and-reborn grain god: the crop represents the deity. Its harvest, which provides food for the people, is his death. Above all, the dismemberment symbolism of these harvest festivals reminds us that they come from ancient shamanic rites that were designed to help the people keep in contact with the spirit world and receive aid and support from it.

In Minoan times, the ordinary people's Feast of Grapes celebrations would have taken place near the vineyards and farms where the grapes were harvested. There were probably also observances at the temple complexes. But it's likely that even for the clergy, the rituals would have been performed outdoors near the temple's vineyards, since the grapevines themselves are such an important symbol. (The temple complexes owned farmland, vineyards, orchards, and livestock whose produce supported the clergy as well as providing emergency stores of food in case of natural disaster.) The Feast of Grapes could be described as a rustic celebration, with a focus on nature and wildness instead of formalized human activities. People would have celebrated in groups ranging in size from a small farm family with just a few people to the huge temple vineyards with their workers, the clergy, and the attending public as well.

The actual harvest in the vineyards may have included ritual components. Maybe someone blessed the crop and thanked the god for his sacrifice before the people began picking the grapes. After the work of the harvest was done, the activities for the Feast of Grapes would have included crushing the grapes to extract their juice (this was done by stomping on them in large wooden vats), feasting and dancing, and pouring libations of wine.

Fig. 10: Detail from the Camp Stool fresco, Knossos

In modern times, the Feast of Grapes can include any kind of grape- or wine-themed food and decorations. This might be a good occasion for a party or feast with like-minded friends or even just a celebratory meal on your own. You might choose background music with an ancient feel, including drums, flutes, and lyres. You could dance if you feel so inclined.

In addition to feasting and dancing, this is a good time for divination. Scrying in bowls of wine is a method that's in keeping with the theme of the festival, but any kind of divination will work. Remember, Dionysus is a shamanic god, so he helps his followers connect with the Underworld and the subconscious. Divination is a good way to access this information, especially if it's done in Dionysus' honor. You could pour him a libation before you begin and ask his help in getting clear answers to your questions.

Bear in mind that it's not necessary to drink wine in order to celebrate the Feast of Grapes. There are many ways to achieve divine ecstasy that don't require alcohol. Dancing or twirling to rhythmic drumming is a good choice and would have been a popular activity in Minoan times. Even children can take part in the dancing and the feasting. In fact, children are pretty good at letting go and achieving mild ecstatic states simply because they want to, so they can set the example and show the adults how to drop their inhibitions and enjoy the day in a way Dionysus would approve of.

The Mysteries

1 through 10 September. The Eleusinian Mysteries appear to have originated on Crete (and possibly on mainland Greece as well) during Minoan times. Back then, the date for the Mysteries each year was based on the heliacal rising of the stars Arcturus and Spica.

The ancient priests and priestesses stood out on their temple rooftops all night long, watching and waiting for the heliacal risings of certain stars so they'd know when the sacred festivals should take place. The two stars they paid attention to for the Mysteries were Arcturus in the constellation Boötes and Spica in the constellation Virgo. These are bright stars that represented two of the deities associated with the Mysteries. Arcturus symbolized Iacchus, an epithet of Dionysus in his youthful form as a boy. Spica was the ear of grain held in the hand of the Mother Goddess (this would have been Rhea for the Minoans and Demeter in the later Greek version of the Eleusinian Mysteries).

In Minoan times, the heliacal rising of Arcturus happened near the beginning of September, and the heliacal rising of Spica occurred ten days later. Today, these two heliacal risings take place about the middle and the end of October. But the timing of the Mysteries didn't move forward with the astronomical changes of these two stars. Instead, during the Bronze Age collapse in the centuries after the fall of Minoan civilization, much of the Minoans' knowledge of astronomy was lost. By the time the Eleusinian Mysteries became a major part of Greek religious practice, the festival had been set on a specific calendar date and no longer had anything to do with the heliacal risings of stars. We've chosen to maintain the Bronze Age dates and to honor the two stars, Arcturus and Spica, even though their heliacal risings no longer take place in September.

The Mysteries center around a mythos that describes the changing seasons and the Mediterranean agricultural cycle. The Greek version is the familiar tale of Persephone being abducted to the Underworld by Hades. Her mother Demeter then searches for her and finally talks Zeus into helping her rescue her daughter. The time when Persephone is held captive in the Underworld is the 'dead' time of year, which is the summer season in the Mediterranean. Persephone's return to the Upperworld heralds the autumn rains and the beginning of the growing season, in other words, the return of life to the world at about the time the Mysteries were enacted every year.

The reconstructed Minoan version of the mythos involves not an abduction, but a voluntary stay in the Underworld. Ariadne, the Queen of the Dead who has access to the Underworld as a regular part of her functions, spends the 'dead' summer season among the Ancestors. After all, she's not needed when the fields lie fallow between growing seasons. As the grain crop embodied, she "dies" at harvest time and descends to the Underworld to stay there for the summer, ministering to the spirits. It's her mother Rhea who stays above, watching the season turn. And it's Rhea who calls Ariadne back when it's time for the rains to come and the crops to grow again.

Ariadne returns to the World Above with the first green sprouts in the autumn fields. Both goddesses take these actions of their own free will, because they recognize their responsibilities and they want to take care of others. The difference in the position of the goddesses in these myths—Ariadne and Rhea as independent characters versus Demeter and Persephone being manipulated by the men—shows just how different the position of women was in Minoan versus Greek society.

Fig. 11: Poppy goddess figurine, Gazi, Crete

While Ariadne is in the Underworld, she's accompanied by her torch-bearer, the goddess Eileithyia. Eileithyia is a midwife-goddess who presides over the liminal times of birth and death. Her torch symbolism was so strong, it continued on into later Greek times, when she was borrowed into the Olympian pantheon. In MMP, we also consider Eileithyia to be the Underworld aspect of the Sun goddess Therasia: the light that travels through the World Below every night, between sunset and sunrise. So she's also Ariadne's light for that goddess' season in the Underworld.

Dionysus is involved in the Mysteries as well, because Rhea isn't an Underworld goddess. She's the Earth Mother, so she needs the help of a deity who can access the Underworld. She asks Dionysus to help her find Ariadne so she can let her daughter know it's time for her to return. This part of the tale eventually becomes the Greek story of young Iacchus (the boy Dionysus) carrying a torch into the Underworld and leading Demeter to her daughter. Iacchus' torch is the star Arcturus, and its heliacal rising told the Minoans that it was time for the Mysteries to begin. There were probably multiple rituals, processions, and other sacred events over the course of the ten-day Mysteries, culminating in the 'big one' at the end.

At the end of the ten-day ritual cycle, Ariadne comes back from the Underworld to take her place once again among the living. In the Mediterranean, autumn is the time for planting the fields. The end of the Mysteries comes shortly before the Autumn Equinox and the beginning of the agricultural cycle. In MMP, we consider that Ariadne comes back with the first green sprouts in the fields of grain. She is the grain crop embodied, her mother's gift to the people.

The Mysteries were popular for centuries because they offer a much deeper message than the simple turning of the seasons. Just as the stars will always rise again at their appointed dates, and just as the seasons will turn and turn again, so the soul continues onward in cycles, never dying, but being renewed from lifetime to lifetime. That's the ultimate symbolism of this mythos, an idea that gave people hope and continued to draw new seekers to the Mysteries until well into the Christian era. That's the secret behind the 'ear of grain reaped in silence' that's so famously associated with this festival (and the Mystery that you can understand in your mind, but that only becomes visceral knowledge when you experience it in ritual). The agricultural cycle and the process of reincarnation are two reflections of the same thing: life turning and returning in a great, silent, sacred circle. As above, so below.

The two ancient versions of the Mysteries (Minoan and Greek) as well as the modern reenactments that some groups put on are large, complex rituals involving lots of people and a big collection of props. Obviously it's not possible to put on such a complicated production if you're a solitary, and it would be tricky with a very small group. But you can still celebrate the Mysteries even if you don't put on the full-blown dramatic version. Devotionals to Rhea,

Ariadne, Eileithyia and Dionysus can help you focus on the deities involved in the Mysteries. Meditating on the story of Ariadne's descent to the Underworld and her return, aided by Eileithyia, Rhea, and Dionysus, is also a good choice. And to get to the core meaning of the Mysteries, you could focus on the concept of cycles, the renewal not just of the seasons but of life itself. You can use some of the items and 'props' listed below to help you focus on these themes.

If you have a group that's large enough to put on a full-scale enactment of the Mysteries, it should be set within the MMP standard ritual format. The mystery play, preferably with interaction from onlookers, becomes the focal point of the Listening section of the ritual. The standard ritual format is described in detail in Chapter 5 and is readily adaptable for any occasion.

Though the Mysteries don't take place at the harvest time of the year for the Mediterranean, they do still have an agricultural theme based around the grain crop. So the kinds of items we associate with the grain harvest—stalks of wheat and baskets of dried grain, for instance—can help set the scene. Underworld-themed objects and artwork can help you focus on that part of the mythos. You might try pomegranates (a food that's sacred to Underworld deities) or photos of caves. The poppy is one of the Underworld goddess' symbols. The Minoans probably used opium as a hallucinogen during rituals. They also grew poppies in their grain fields as a reminder of the Underworld associations of the two plants. An image of a torch could stand for Eileithyia accompanying Ariadne and/or Iacchus leading Rhea through the Underworld, and also for the idea of enlightenment and joy (but please don't try to use a real torch indoors!).

The New Year

Autumn Equinox, approximately 21 September. The new year in the Mediterranean agricultural cycle happens in the autumn when the rainy season starts again after a long, hot, dry summer. The agricultural cycle is its own thing, overlapping only partly with the sailing season. In ancient Crete, people probably considered themselves either sea-oriented (sailors, traders, and their families) or land-oriented (farmers and their families). In the modern world, we have the luxury of incorporating both cycles into our spiritual lives.

During the height of Minoan civilization, the temple complexes probably held the agricultural new year's celebrations on the exact date of the Equinox since they had the ability to calculate the date based on their astronomical observations. But the Minoan farmers and other ordinary people probably did their real celebrating when the rains actually began, and that date would have varied from year to year. The festivities throughout Crete would have taken place outdoors at local farms, peak sanctuaries, and along the banks of the newly-invigorated rivers and creeks as a way to connect with the renewal of the natural cycle.

Fig. 12: Pitcher with vegetative labryses, Knossos

The agricultural new year is the beginning of the green-and-growing season. You can celebrate this festival whenever the appropriate time occurs in the region where you live, whether that's the spring or the autumn. If you live very far north, your 'real spring' might not begin until weeks after the Spring Equinox, but that's all right. This is a nature religion, so cuing in to Earth's cycles where you live is the most important thing.

The Autumn Equinox was a celebratory time for the Minoans, the end of the long holiday season that began with the Feast of Grapes and continued with the Mysteries. Once the rainy season began each autumn, the soil was finally soft enough that the farmers could plow their fields and plant their crops. To this day, farmers in the Mediterranean plant their crops in the autumn, though they don't plow the fields with oxen anymore. This is a time to celebrate the renewal of life and the promise of abundance to come, as the new crops are planted and begin to grow.

When the Autumn Equinox came each year, the Minoans would have just finished celebrating Ariadne's return from the Underworld, so she's an important part of the new year's festivities. But so is Rhea since she's Mother Earth, the land that receives the rain and in whose rich soil the crops will grow to nourish the people for another year.

We can turn to the same kinds of items and symbols for this celebration that we usually associate with spring in the northern temperate zone: fresh flowers and herbs in bouquets, garlands, and wreaths, and also as necklaces, crowns, and hair decorations. Colorful ribbons can add to the festive air as well. One common activity that can really evoke the feeling of the new growing season is to plant some quick-sprouting seeds like lettuce or wheatgrass in a small container and watch them grow, fresh and green. For a stronger 'new life' vibe, you can use empty eggshells as your containers for growing the new sprouts. And of course, any of the symbols and objects associated with the deities for this festival would make good additions to your sacred space.

Harbor Home

Third Monday of October. Harbor Home takes place around the time of year that the Pleiades had their heliacal setting in Minoan times. It marks the end of the sailing season, the time of year when the ships all came home to their harbors and were put in storage for the winter, to be repaired and readied for the next season. Just as farmers rested and repaired their tools in the off season, sailors and traders did the same. The winter winds in the Mediterranean made it dangerous for sailing after a certain point in the autumn, so the ships came back to harbor for a few months every year.

Once again, we're not sure what the Minoans did in terms of honoring this time of year, but it's a good bet they marked the occasion somehow, giving thanks for the safe return of the ships and their crews. Ship's captains would have known to be back in harbor by the time of the heliacal setting of the Pleiades, both for their own safety and so they could take part in whatever kind of ceremony the people traditionally held. Having a return time for the ships would also have provided a sense of security for those who stayed behind, knowing that family members and friends would be back by a certain point in the year. Considering that a sizeable portion of the Minoan population probably left to go sailing and trading every year, this must have been pretty important.

Of course, there were probably people who didn't make it home. If they died on board ship, they would have been given burial at sea. Some traders may have been taken ill in foreign lands and died there. Given the lack of any way to preserve a corpse back then, it's unlikely the body would have been brought back home. They would probably have been buried wherever they died. So the crew members who returned with the ship would have had to bring the bad news to the family. This means that Harbor Home would have incorporated a mourning aspect as well as a celebratory one. It was very different back then; you wouldn't know until the end of the sailing season whether your family members and friends were alive and well. So seeing them arrive safely home would have been a profoundly moving experience.

Based on the probable ending of the sailing season in Minoan times, we've set Harbor Home on the third Monday in October. That's about when the heliacal setting of the Pleiades occurred in the late Bronze Age. And if you're lucky enough to be able to take the day off work as a religious holiday, you get a three-day weekend. Like this festival's springtime counterpart the Blessing of the Ships, the date for this one makes it a *floating holiday*—very appropriate for a festival that focuses on ships and sailing!

Fig. 13: Akrotiri town and harbor, fresco detail, Akrotiri

If you have a boat (or a surfboard or jet ski) you can perform a Harbor Home ceremony at the end of the season. As with the Blessing of the Ships, you should start with an offering to Posidaeja. Her preferred libation is pure water from a natural source, but wine is appropriate for this festival as well, more than for any other occasion associated with Grandmother Ocean. Use white wine for celebratory ritual and red wine if there's a mourning component to your Harbor Home. If you're offering wine, be sure to pour it into a bowl or onto the ground and not into the water. If there's a mourning component to your rite, you can set up a small altar to honor the person or persons who passed away.

It's also appropriate to offer a small object that you value but that won't do any harm to the water when you throw it in. What you choose will depend on the content of this occasion in any particular year. If you're giving thanks for a safe and enjoyable sailing season, a semiprecious stone in shades of clear, white, or blue or perhaps a few pieces of sea glass would be appropriate. If you're mourning injury, damage, or death, a small item you associate with the deceased person or damaged ship is a good choice. If you're decommissioning a boat or other water craft, you can offer a small piece of it, as long as it's not harmful (no heavy metals, lead paint, etc.). Ships have long been considered as quasi-living things; that's why they're given names. So taking one out of service can be viewed as a funeral of sorts.

As with the Blessing of the Ships, fresh flowers are appropriate here, whether your Harbor Home involves celebration or mourning or both. Loose flowers, garlands, and wreaths will all work. Just be sure, if you're making garlands or wreaths, that all the materials are fully biodegradable. You could also make daisy chain style floral decorations, since they don't require any materials except the flowers themselves. Make the offering by tossing the flowers into the water.

Once you've made your offering, it's time to ask Posidaeja's blessing and to give thanks for the end of the season. Scoop up some water from the lake, river, or ocean and pour it over the prow of the boat. You can also brew some herb-infused water (herb tea, essentially) from rosemary, rue, sage, or myrtle and sprinkle that to bless your boat. If there's a mourning aspect to your Harbor Home ceremony, you can also take this time to say a few words about that part of the season.

For a group ritual among several friends who have boats, decorate your water craft with garlands and streamers. Have a ceremonial procession across the water, ending up back at the harbor, and perform your ritual after everyone has docked. This should take place at the end of boating season, so it should be the last time any of you go out on the water until the next season.

Of course, not everyone lives near the water or owns a boat. So, just like with the Blessing of the Ships, we can repurpose Harbor Home as a ceremony to end a long journey or summer vacation season, in which case it might take place on a date other than the third Monday in October. Make your offerings as outlined above. Use the water-pouring or sprinkling part of the ritual to bless your car, RV, bicycle, hiking gear, and so on, as well as the people involved, or to vicariously bless an airplane, train, or bus via a printout of your ticket. Then give thanks for your safe return and mourn any losses that happened along the way.

The Depths of Winter

Winter Solstice, approximately 21 December. This festival has two layers in MMP, one that focuses on our Sun goddess Therasia and one that centers around Rhea and her Divine Child. In both cases, the central symbolism is that of birth and rebirth, of the old cycle ending and a new one beginning. Minoan civilization lasted for many centuries, and during that time religion changed and grew. Like the Egyptians, the Minoans tended to simply add new ideas, gods, and celebrations on top of what was already there instead of substituting the new ones and removing older ones. So over time, Minoan religion became a lot more complicated, with multiple reflections of the same ideas throughout the sacred year. We've included some of these nuanced layers in our sacred calendar because they have meaning for us as modern Pagan practitioners.

As the Sun in divine form, Therasia's power grows over the course of the year, reaching its scorching hot peak at the Summer Solstice. From there, her strength slowly wanes until, at the Winter Solstice, she's so weak that she retreats into her cave. For three days she remains there, hidden, dying, dead. Then she's reborn, like the Phoenix that burns itself up and arises from its own ashes. She emerges from the cave fresh and new, ready to begin the cycle again. Her sacred colors of blood-red and gold fit in nicely with modern notions of what Winter Solstice decorations ought to look like. Remember that the blood-red color comes from the precious murex dye and the gold comes from saffron, another substance that's sacred to Therasia.

The second myth we use to celebrate the Winter Solstice is the story of Rhea, the Great Mother Goddess, giving birth to the Divine Child Dionysus. Dionysus isn't a Sun god but a year-king, an embodiment of the solar year. We think this festival became a major part of the sacred calendar late in Minoan times and was a kind of additional new year, in addition to the agricultural new year in the autumn and the opening of the sailing season in the late spring.

Like modern Pagans from many different traditions, the Minoans probably kept vigil overnight the night before Winter Solstice, waiting for the moment of the sunrise. The clergy used the flat rooftops of the temple complexes as observatory platforms and may have used the sacred horns that lined the roof edges as sighting markers. During the Summer Solstice, the peak sanctuaries would also have served as excellent observatories to view the coming sunrise, but they were inaccessible during the winter so the temple rooftops would have had to do. When the temple astronomers spotted the first glimmer of the Winter Solstice sunrise on the southeastern horizon, they would have made some sort of signal to notify the people. We don't know exactly what this was, but it may have involved lighting torches or fires on the temple rooftops along with blowing conch shell trumpets.

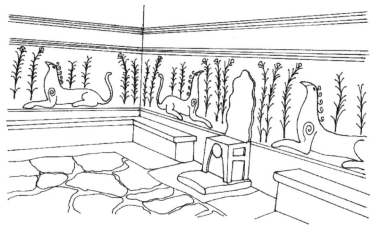

Fig. 14: Throne Room, Knossos temple complex

I believe the so-called Throne Room in the Knossos temple complex was the scene of a ritual re-enactment of Dionysus' birth each year at Winter Solstice. The Throne Room has several sunrise alignments, including one at Winter Solstice: the rising Sun shines in a direct line through the anteroom and illuminates the throne, the seat that archaeologists now say was used not by a king but by a priestess. In the MMP mythos, it's Rhea's birthing chair. Just imagine what it would have been like to be among the select few to witness this event, a priestess enacting the part of the pregnant Mother Goddess Rhea in labor, with the baby being born just as the newborn Sun shines a spotlight on that special place.

This festival is familiar to many of us in the modern world since we're accustomed to seeing celebrations of the birth of a divine child (in Christian terms) or the rebirth of the Sun (in Pagan terms) at Midwinter. Throughout the ages there have been many variants on this story, but the Minoan version is the oldest one we've discovered so far. Dionysus' birth was celebrated in the towns and temple complexes but also at the cave shrines, since it's in her sacred cave that Rhea gives birth to her son. Rhea was probably not honored at the peak sanctuaries at Winter Solstice, since traveling up the mountainsides at this time of year was dangerous if not impossible (the mountain peaks in Crete are covered with snow and ice in winter). But the caves were low enough down that they continued to be accessible year-round.

Dionysus' birth includes many of the bits we're familiar with at this time of year: a sacred mother giving birth to a son without a father; friendly animals (the Horned Ones, particularly Amalthea) surrounding the birth scene; the birth happening in a cave or grotto; the child being hidden away for safety; the child being worshiped. In Dionysus' case, we also have the sacred pine or fir tree that he's associated with. This is the shamanic World Tree that connects the realms. It's via this tree that the soul of the newborn comes into this world from the land of the Ancestors. Some versions of the story even include a bright star shining above the tree to show that Dionysus has come. Sound familiar?

Decorations for this festival would have looked pretty familiar to us. Evergreens of all sorts, in garlands and swags, would have hung on homes, businesses, and the temple complexes both indoors and out. Sun symbols would have been a part of the trimmings as well. But unlike our modern red/green/gold color scheme that's so popular for the winter holiday season, we think the Minoans focused on purple and gold, the color of the grape (Dionysus' sacred fruit) and the Sun. You could add in some green for the evergreen pine and fir if you like.

We have no evidence for Minoan-era nativity scenes, but I see no reason not to include one in our modern version of this holy day. A nativity scene that looks like a cave or grotto setting would be most appropriate, along with the Sacred Mother, the Divine Child, and the Friendly Beasts. Of course, you should keep the Divine Child hidden until after sunrise on Solstice morning, at which point he should magically appear on the scene.

The Blessing of the Waters

January 6 or the first full Moon after Winter Solstice. This festival in our sacred calendar derives from a local Christian holy day, a thinly-veiled remnant of an ancient practice that has survived the centuries in Crete. The rite appears to have evolved from a much older one that involved blessing the spirits of streams, lakes, and other bodies of water, including possibly the sea. Dance ethnography suggests that this might also have been one way, in pre-Christian times, for people to celebrate the coming-of-age of young men and possibly to choose a particular young man for a special religious office.

Why should we have a whole festival dedicated just to water? Let's be honest: those of us who live in modern developed countries are kind of spoiled about water. All we have to do is turn on a tap to get all we want, hot or cold, perfectly safe to drink. Now granted, the Minoans were pretty high-tech for their time. They had aqueducts that brought water into the cities and towns from Crete's mountain springs, and they dug canals to bring water to their fields. Even so, many people still had to lug their water around in buckets. People probably still got sick from bad water on occasion. And the Minoans knew that in bad years, the springs would all but dry up in the summer, leaving them to hope they had stored enough rainwater in their cisterns to make it through until the rains started up again in the autumn. So we want to honor the water, wherever it comes from in our daily lives. We can't live without it, and the water cycle on Earth is closed. This is all the water we have.

Fig. 15: River scene fresco, Akrotiri

We've set the date for the Blessing of the Waters in January or possibly late December. For those who don't mind overlapping with the Christian calendar, Epiphany (6 January) is the date of the modern Cretan festival. There's some evidence that these rites were originally associated with the Winter Solstice, so the first full Moon after Solstice, whether it falls in December or January, is another option.

What do we do to celebrate this rite? We go to the nearest body of water, whether that's a stream, pond, lake, river, or the ocean. If you live in a land-locked area with no natural water nearby, you could set out a bowl to catch rain water and use that. Failing that, water from your tap will work. But don't use bottled water, even if it's natural spring water, because it's not local—it was imported from far away, and the point of this rite is to get in touch with your local water.

Because the purpose of this rite is to express gratitude for the water that's so vital for life on Earth, we make offerings at the shore or bank of the body of water, or in front of an altar that holds a bowl of local water. Appropriate offerings for this rite include incense, a chant or song, and food that would be safe for the wildlife in the area (birdseed, for instance, as long as it doesn't contain the seeds of invasive species). After making the offering, we touch the water and thank it, telling it how much we value it. Then we touch the water to ourselves to complete the connection.

You can anoint your forehead with the water, for instance. If you're doing the rite in a group, the leader can sprinkle the water lightly over all the participants. A small bunch of fresh herbs makes a great tool for this (it's called an aspergillum).

This rite can also be used as a coming-of-age ceremony for boys, though obviously if you're going to have a young man jump into the water in January, you want to be sure he's healthy enough for it to be safe, and have plenty of blankets and hot drinks on hand for afterward if you live in the part of the world where January is wintertime. While the Christian version involves throwing a cross into the water to be retrieved, we think tossing a labrys would be a good choice. The ritual leader or perhaps the boy's parents can throw the item into the water. He demonstrates his adulthood by leaping into the water, grabbing the object, and bringing it back out. Again, making offerings to the spirit of the water and thanking it for its value in your life should also be a part of this rite. The young man can make the first offering, introducing himself to the spirit of the water.

If you're feeling intrepid, you could also use this rite the way we think it might have been used in ancient times, to choose a special young man for some sacred office. Thankfully, human sacrifice is out of fashion, but if you're looking for a dramatic way to pick a priest for your Pagan group, this fits the bill. Instead of tossing an item in the water and having one young man retrieve it, you would gather a group of young men on the bank or shore. Toss the item into the water, then have all the young men jump in and go for the item. Whoever gets it and brings it back to shore is the winner.

Harvest Festival and Feast of the Dead

Spring Equinox, approximately 21 March. The crops were sown half a year ago in the autumn when the rainy season began. They've grown throughout the mild winter and are now ready to be harvested. This festival is for the grain crops, since the vegetables would have been harvested at different times throughout the growing season as they came ripe. Also, grain needs special processing and preparation before it can be used, and this processing (threshing and winnowing) was part of the harvest activities. Since Ariadne is the embodiment of the grain crop, the harvest represents her death and descent to the Underworld for the next portion of the year.

Like the Feast of Grapes, the actual harvest activities in the ancient world would have taken place when the crops were ready. This date would have varied from year to year and might have been different from one type of grain to another. The Minoans grew barley and several different types of wheat. It's possible the temple clergy had some sort of official celebration on the actual date of Spring Equinox. We know they calculated the Equinox dates carefully each year through observation of the Sun's movements. But the farmers would have held their celebrations at the actual harvest, whenever that was.

When the grain was ready to harvest, the people of ancient Crete would cut the stalks with bronze sickles and carry them to the threshing floors. These were large, circular outdoor areas that were either paved with flat stones or covered with tightly-packed soil. They would spread the grain stalks out on the threshing floor and either drive their animals (oxen or goats) around in circles over the stalks, or the people themselves would trample the grain. This process breaks the seed heads apart and gets the grain kernels loose from the stalks. While the people stomped the grain, they would sing and chant to make the time pass faster. It's this harvest-time activity that eventually led to the first circle dances. The celebratory chants and dances took place after the grain processing was finished and the harvest was removed from the threshing floor.

The threshing-floor dances would have been performed in thanks to the ancestors for the abundant harvest. The Minoans probably envisioned the crop growing up from the Underworld with the ancestors' aid after the seeds had been planted in the Earth. These circular dances on the threshing floor were originally shamanic in nature and were probably the origin of the Crane Dance and possibly related to the concept of walking the labyrinth. During these dances, members of the clergy may have made shamanic journeys to the Underworld to directly thank the ancestors for their gifts. Everyone who participated would have entered a light trance state simply because of the rhythmic nature of the activity. In MMP, we thank not only the spirits of the dead but also Ariadne, the Queen of the Dead and Lady of the Labyrinth, who gives herself in the form of the grain crop for our sustenance.

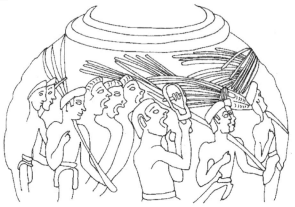

Fig. 16: Harvester vase, Hagia Triada

In addition to the dances on the threshing floors, the Minoans also feasted at the tombs of their ancestors to celebrate the harvest. The big tholos (beehive-shaped) tombs in Crete had paved plazas in front of them where these communal feasts were held. The ancestors would have been honored guests at the feast, making this event a Feast of the Dead as well as a harvest celebration. It would be typical of ancient grain harvest celebrations for the Minoans to make bread or porridge from the first grain that was harvested. This 'first fruits' dish would have been a special offering to the ancestors at the tombs. Offerings of all the food and drink from the feast were left at the tomb entrances. The people also drank toasts to the ancestors and the gods. One interesting practice they had was, we think, designed to prove they had drunk the whole toast or poured out the full libation: they would turn the cup upside down and leave it, or sometimes they would even smash the cup on the ground in front of the tomb.

Depending on the climate and the seasons where you live, it might make more sense to celebrate this harvest festival at the Autumn Equinox instead of the in the spring. One important aspect of Paganism is honoring the Earth wherever we happen to live. Of course, unless you're actually harvesting a crop, it's probably easiest to celebrate on the Equinox itself (or on the nearest available weekend, which seems to be the way many of us modern folks with nine-to-five jobs have do it). It's perfectly all right to reverse the two equinox celebrations in our sacred calendar to match the seasons where you live. Just don't switch any of the other festival dates.

Harvest decorations like stalks, sheaves of grain, and loaves of bread are appropriate here. Since this isn't just a harvest festival but also a Feast of the Dead, the color red has its place, the color of the ancestors and the Underworld. You could cook a special meal, perhaps one that you share with family or friends, in honor of the good things you've 'harvested' over the course of the year and also in honor of your ancestors. Freshly-baked bread would be a good choice, as would any kind of naturally red food in honor of the Blessed Dead.

In addition to the ancestors, this is a time to honor Ariadne and the Melissae, who are the guardians of the Underworld. Offerings of grain (plain or cooked into bread), red and yellow flowers, incense, honey, and poppyseed are appropriate. You certainly don't have to smash your cup after you offer a toast to the ancestors, but turning it upside down on the table is a good way to show that you've drained it in their honor.

Chapter 5:
The Rituals

Obviously, the point of a spiritual practice is that you actually *practice* it. This chapter will give you some ideas for arranging your sacred space and getting started with the standard MMP ritual format.

As you move along your personal spiritual path, be sure to listen to your inner voice. Set up your altar the way that feels right to you. Listen for the gods' answers to your questions. Your spiritual practice should add depth and meaning to your life, not make you feel like you have 'one more thing to get over with' before you can go do something else. You should also be aware that, generally speaking, MMP is a path of active engagement with the divine in daily life. While everyone needs a certain amount of alone time for contemplation, we don't withdraw from the world, but participate in it.

Setting Up Your Sacred Space

We all want to 'do it right' when it comes to our spirituality, but when it comes down to the details, it doesn't really matter where you do what you do in Modern Minoan Paganism. You don't need to have a temple or a covenstead or a separate room dedicated to spiritual work. In fact, you don't even need a permanent altar. You can set up your altar each time you want to do a ritual—on your desk or the kitchen table or some other convenient surface—then take it down afterward and store the items someplace safe until next time. In other words, you should do whatever you need to so you can fit your unique spirituality into your unique life. This isn't a one-size-fits-all kind of situation.

The important thing is that you take the time, on a regular basis, to follow the spiritual practice that's right for you and that fulfills your needs.

If it works for you, you might choose to have an altar set up permanently. Depending on your living arrangements, you might be able to do this in a public area like a living room, or you might need to confine it to your private space like a bedroom. In the living room, a bookshelf or fireplace mantel is a good spot for an altar, since it's not likely to be disturbed like it would be on a more accessible surface like a coffee table (feline roommates notwithstanding). My non-Pagan friends think I have 'interesting knick-knacks' on my fireplace mantel and bookshelves. Little do they know! In a bedroom, most people have a dresser or chest of drawers where they pile their stuff. This is a good spot for an altar because you already consider it your territory. Simply clear it off and set up your altar. Just be sure to respect it as sacred space. Don't dump your keys and your spare change on it when you get home in the evening.

It's a good idea to have your purpose in mind before you begin arranging your altar. Will this be a devotional to one or more deities? Is it a celebration of Minoan spirituality in general? Do you intend to do particular rituals toward a goal like prosperity, protection, or romance? Focus on your purpose and let it roll around in your mind as you gather the items you'll be including in your sacred space.

Many of us like to define our altar space with a cloth as the base layer. Now, we don't know for sure how the Minoans used fabric in their shrines and altars because it has all disintegrated after so many centuries. This is where we get to fill in the blanks with practices that make sense for us in the modern world. If you like the idea of an altar cloth to delineate your sacred space, then use one. An altar cloth can be virtually anything that works as a base layer: a scarf, a placemat, a plain piece of fabric. In fact, it doesn't even have to be a cloth. I've used baskets and platters as the base for altars, and I have a friend who likes seagrass and bamboo mats. Choose whatever feels right to you, bearing in mind the preferences of any deities you'll be including on the altar. I like to allow myself to drift into a light meditative state when I'm setting up my sacred space. That way, I can sense my intuition more clearly and make choices that will work well for my purpose and my relationship with the gods.

Like everyone else in the ancient world, the Minoans used oil lamps to light their living and working spaces. Candles hadn't been invented yet. But in our modern world, candles are a lot easier to find than oil lamps, and far less likely to make a mess if you tip them over. If you want to search out an ancient-style oil lamp from a museum shop or online supplier, you certainly can (fill it with olive oil to be authentic). Indian markets also commonly carry oil lamps in the autumn, around the time of Diwali. But since we're living in the modern world, in most cases it's all right to use candles instead. Their flame still evokes the feel of ancient times, and they're readily available. You can use plain white candles or choose shapes and colors that add to the feeling and focus you're aiming to create with your altar. In MMP, we have a few deities who prefer oil lamps rather than candles, so check those details in Chapter 3 if you're planning to develop a relationship with those gods and goddesses. But generally speaking, candles are just fine.

Once you've chosen your spot and your altar cloth (if you're using one), simply add the other items until it feels right to you. We have no way of knowing whether the Minoans had rules about where items went in shrines or altars, so it's best to simply arrange your altar accoutrements in a way that pleases you. Do your best to listen to your inner voice when choosing items and arranging them in your sacred space. Decide what to put on your altar based on its focus or purpose. If you're honoring a god or goddess (or more than one), pick symbols, objects, and colors associated with them. If you want a general Minoan altar, choose a combination of items that symbolize the ancient Minoans and their spirituality to you.

Make sure you're comfortable with the arrangement you've created before you do a ritual or meditation with the altar. If your sacred space feels like it's missing something, try meditating in front of the altar and asking what else you need. Once you've figured out what's missing, go get it! Thankfully, in this age of supermarkets, craft shops, and Internet shopping, it's not usually difficult to find or make the bits and pieces you need to fill out your sacred space. We've found that the deities in our pantheon are especially appreciative of items we make ourselves, since we're putting in extra effort in our relationship with them and practicing handcrafts like so many artisans did in ancient Crete.

If your altar setup is temporary, it's a good idea to organize some storage space for your sacred items while you're putting the altar together. That way it will be easy to put your altar back together the next time you want it, and you won't have to worry about losing anything that's dear to you. Choose the amount of storage space you'll need based on the items you'll be including on your altar. A little room in a closet or a chest of drawers, or even under a bed, should work just fine unless you have some really big figurines or candlesticks. Avoid damp basements and garages unless you enjoy discovering that your favorite altar cloth is covered in mold. And be sure the other members of your household know your sacred wares are not to be disturbed. If they're not likely to respect your items, an undisclosed hiding spot is a good idea. It also pays to use sturdy boxes or other containers to store your altar stuff so it will be safe and you won't open a closet door to find the broken pieces of your favorite figurine on the floor.

Now that you have your altar set up, you're ready to do a ritual, right? Not exactly. Let's take a few precautions first. Even if you're practicing alone, you might not actually *be* alone. If there are other people (or disruptive pets) in your household, make arrangements with them before beginning rituals or meditation. If you're constantly worried that you'll be interrupted, you won't be able to relax and get into the swing of things. And the last thing you want is a cat jumping up on an altar and knocking over your lit candles so your altar cloth catches fire (ask me how I know this). But if you're assured of quiet space and time, you can focus on your spiritual activities and get more out of them. And of course, be sure to turn off your phone, the TV, and any other electronics that are liable to disrupt you. This is an easy one to forget. Even those of us who've been practicing for years can attest to remembering to turn the phone off only after it rings right in the middle of a ritual!

If you're doing a formal ritual and not a casual, off-the-cuff one, a bit of helpful advice I've learned over the years is to read the ritual through completely and be sure you understand the whole thing before you begin. This is pretty much the same as reading a recipe through completely before you start cooking. You need to understand the process and make sure you have all the ingredients on hand before you start so you don't find yourself halfway through, panicking that you're all out of something-or-other. So take your time to prepare, and you'll experience a more enjoyable and meaningful ritual. Our standard ritual format works for a wide variety of situations. Once you've used it a few times, it will be familiar and you won't need to go over it in much detail except for the parts that you specialize for your ritual occasion. If you like, you can use it the first time to consecrate your altar. That special ritual comes right after the standard format, further down in this chapter.

Bear in mind, the Minoans lived centuries (millennia, actually) before the kind of ceremonial magic that's the basis of Wicca and related modern Pagan traditions. Like the rest of the ancient world, the Minoans had permanent temples and shrines that were consecrated when they were first constructed and then re-sacralized from time to time during ritual. We don't use Wiccan-style circle casting or quarter calls in MMP. Instead, our ritual format is based on the archaeological evidence from ancient Crete and comparative research with other Bronze Age religions from the eastern Mediterranean and Near East.

In MMP, you can perform rituals indoors or outdoors, whatever works in terms of your ritual purpose and site availability. The Minoans apparently did both. It's a good idea to make sure the location and terrain are accessible for all the participants, and to have a sheltered location available as an option for outdoor rituals in case of inclement weather.

Every ritual should have a specific purpose. This might include celebration of one of the festivals in the sacred calendar, giving thanks for blessings received, a request for help or healing from the divine, or dedicating an altar. You should choose deities that are appropriate to the ritual's purpose, bearing in mind your own relationships with any of the Minoan gods and goddesses. Some of them have specialties, so to speak, but often it's best to work with the ones you've developed a strong connection with.

MMP is meant to be accessible to everyone. It's OK to make modifications to the ritual format to accommodate accessibility issues as long as you don't omit any of the six major sections (Preparing, Inviting, Welcoming, Offering, Listening, Returning). Also, sign language is a perfectly acceptable method of speaking any of the parts in a MMP ritual, including any of the chants.

In a group ritual, you can share out the spoken parts as you like, beyond just the presiding clergy. This helps spread out the workload and gives more people the opportunity to actively participate in the rite. For our purposes here, the term "clergy" includes everyone who will take an active role in the presentation of the ritual: the people who have speaking parts, the people who lead any singing and dancing, and the people who perform instrumental music. We prefer the term "clergy" to priest or priestess because it's a non-gendered term and allows for the inclusion of people who don't fit into the gender binary.

The clergy who'll be performing the rite should set up the altar before the ritual begins. Here's something that's probably different from what you're used to: the altar shouldn't have any figurines or other representations of the deities on it to begin with. These will be brought in during the procession and placed on the altar at the beginning of the ritual. I'll refer to them as figurines below, but other representations of the deities are acceptable (a seashell for Posidaeja, for instance, or a thyrsus for Dionysus—see Chapter 3 for more ideas).

You should also have a second small table near the altar; we'll call it the side table. It will hold the offerings until it's time to give them to the deities during the ritual, and it's the place you'll set the trays and baskets you used to bring the deity figurines into the ritual area. It's also where you should set any items you'll need for the ritual that don't belong on the altar, like matches or a lighter. If you'll be performing a mystery play or any other activity that will need props, put them on the side table so they'll be ready to use at the appropriate point during the ritual. Be sure to put them back on the table when you're done with them.

Bear in mind that items may feel different to you after you use them in a ritual. The deity figurines, libation bowls, incense burners, and any other object you have on the altar will be affected by the energy that's raised during the ritual. In a sense, the objects on your altar will "wake up" during the ritual and become part of the temple that the ritual creates. This can even include your altar cloth and the tabletop. It's important to recognize that this can happen and treat the items on your altar with care and reverence. Following the standard ritual format provides a smooth way to enliven these objects and then request that they return to their regular state afterward. In some cases you may find that objects used as deity figurines retain some "liveliness" after a ritual due to the residue of the deity within them. If this happens, you can consider that the deity has personally consecrated your figurine, so you should treat it with respect and thank the deity for the honor.

As you're getting ready for a ritual, if you feel the area is in need of cleansing, you can asperge it with plain water, salt water, or herb water before beginning the rite. Participants can also be asperged before the ritual begins. This is easiest to do as people line up for the procession. This can be a helpful way of releasing the stresses and thoughts of the day and turning toward the focus of the ritual. In MMP, incense is used as an offering, not a method of purification or consecration, so asperge instead to clear your ritual area.

If you're going to have deity figurines on the altar for the rite, they should be carried in during the procession, preferably not in bare hands, but on trays or in shallow baskets—in other words, they don't start out on the altar, even if that's where they'll be during the ritual. It's respectful to keep the figurines covered with a basket lid or a soft cloth until the time of the procession, at which point the covers will be taken off. Be sure to organize the deity figurines and their containers or trays before you start the ritual.

In MMP, we don't order the deities around in any way. We invite them in via the processional and welcome them once we (and they) are in the ritual space together. Their presence consecrates the ritual space, so there's no need for circle casting or any similar activity. As I mentioned above, our tradition is not based on Wicca and its practices.

You should arrange the offerings on the side table before the ritual begins. This is considered part of setting up the altar and ritual space. During the ritual, you should actively pour out liquid offerings (libations) and not just set them out in a container. It's the act of pouring that turns an ordinary liquid into a sacred offering. For outdoor rituals, you can pour libations on the ground. For both indoor and outdoor rituals, you can pour libations into a container like a bowl or libation table that's sitting on the altar.

When you're choosing the offerings for a ritual, bear in mind the preferences of the deities you're giving the gift to. Check Chapter 3 for the specifics of what each deity does and doesn't like. If you're putting on a group ritual, one of the clergy members should be in charge of the offerings. They should choose which offerings to use and will be responsible for responding to the deities during the ritual if they turn out to be unhappy with the offerings (don't panic—that's very unlikely as long as you've followed the guidelines in the listings for the deities and the sacred calendar). You should decide on all the offerings before the ritual starts. If non-clergy want to contribute offerings to a group ritual, they should let the clergy member who's in charge of the offerings know ahead of time, to make sure they've made an appropriate choice.

MMP group rituals include clergy who "embody" the deities during ritual. This can be as simple as speaking pre-written or extemporaneous lines as if the clergy member were the deity — this is the most common method of embodying. But it can also involve trance possession of the clergy member by the deity. Trance possession should be undertaken only by people who have the training and experience to do so safely. Trance possession is NOT necessary in order to create a moving and meaningful ritual, so please don't experiment if you don't know what you're doing. Our deities aren't malicious, but they are quite powerful, and their presence can do unintentional harm to people who don't have the proper training. Check the resources in Chapter 9 if you'd like to find out more about trance possession and how to do it safely.

The garments the clergy who are embodying the deities wear are a way of inviting and welcoming the deities into the ritual. The sincerity with which you choose and create your ritual outfits matters here because the deities can sense it. The symbols, colors, and materials also matter because each deity has preferences, the same way that humans prefer certain styles, colors, and fabrics over others. Check Chapter 3 for more details. The most important aspect here is sincerity — just do your best and the deities will recognize that. The one requirement is that if Ourania will be a part of your rite, whoever embodies her should have their face covered. This is usually done with a black or grey veil, since Ourania is "beyond" the Three Mothers and isn't as easily anthropomorphized. She is the cosmos itself.

Though the Mothers are always invited first in any ritual, it's not necessary to have clergy embody them every time. It's only necessary to have clergy embody the main deities who are the focus of the ritual (for instance, Posidaeja at the Blessing of the Waters or Ariadne and the Melissae at a ritual to honor the spirits of the dead).

MMP rituals begin and end with processions accompanied by chants. In group rituals, it can be helpful to designate a person to lead the chants. That way, those who are unfamiliar with the chants will have a confident voice to lead them, and the chant leader can provide a clear beginning and ending for each chant, especially if it's going to be repeated.

Remember that all the parts of the ritual process, from planning and preparing to enacting to cleaning up afterward, should be completed reverently and with humility. It's all part of the sacred act of performing a ritual. We're spending time, energy, materials and attention to connect with the divine. We get the best results, in terms of everyone's experience in the ritual and our relationship with the deities, when we complete every stage of the process in a way that's respectful to both the divine and the human participants. Preparing mindfully and reverently also makes the temple ready to be respectfully put to rest (for permanent temple spaces) or disassembled (for temporary ritual spaces) once the rite is over. We do our best always to show the deities and our fellow human beings the appropriate respect by being mindful as we work our way through the process. Note, however, that mindful doesn't necessarily mean somber: joy is sacred, too. Just bear in mind that there's a difference between keeping a sense of humor and ridiculing or disparaging what's going on.

Group Ritual Format
<u>Preparing</u>
In this stage we transform a space that might have been used for other activities into a temple. We do this by "awakening" the space and the items that will be used in the ritual. This means we're opening the location, the objects, and the clergy to the presence of the divine so they can serve as welcoming hosts for both the deities and the humans who will take part in the rite. This applies equally to permanent altar/temple spaces and temporary ones like public parks.

For group rituals, be sure to have seating outside the ritual space for people who are waiting, as well as within the ritual space for those who need it. Bear in mind other aspects of accessibility as you're designing your ritual, so that people with movement, hearing, vision, or other issues can have a full and meaningful experience.

The size and shape of the ritual space should be appropriate for the number of people and the activities that will be included in the rite (dancing, for instance). Since we don't cast circles in MMP, the ritual space can be rectangular or any other shape that works for the location. Just be sure that all participants can see the altar during the ritual, and try to provide enough room that people don't feel cramped or confined.

Prepare the altar and the side table beforehand, allowing only those who are setting it up to enter the ritual space. Others should wait outside. The altar should be set up by some or all of the clergy who will be performing the rite. It's preferable, but not mandatory, to have the ritual area be out of sight of the people who are waiting. After the ritual is over, the altar and ritual area should still be treated with respect. While the clean-up and dismantling process can include anyone who wishes to help (it's always good to have help!), the clergy who set up the altar should guide the process. After all, they're the ones who know what goes where.

Once the altar is ready, everyone gathers outside the ritual space and lines up for the procession. For a group ritual, participants line up behind the clergy. Any clergy who will embody deities during the ritual go first, in order of precedence: the Mothers always go first, followed by any other deities involved in the rite.

The procession itself can be single-file or with several people abreast, whatever suits your ritual space. The clergy member who will embody each deity can carry their deity's figurine, or someone else can take on that task. Asking non-clergy to carry the deities in the processional is a good way to encourage participation and help everyone feel like they're an integral part of the group. If someone other than the embodying clergy member carries a deity's figurine, they should stand right beside or behind the embodying clergy member in the procession so they're sort of a single unit, if you see what I mean.

If you're going to asperge the participants, now is the time to do it, while everyone is lined up and waiting for the ritual to start. Have one clergy member very lightly sprinkle the water (or herb-water or salt water) on themselves, then go down the line and asperge everyone, beginning with the clergy, on through to the end of the line. Then they put away the water and get back into line so the ritual can begin.

It's a good idea to ask people to turn their phones off at this point. It's very unpleasant to have a phone sound off in the middle of the ritual and break the mood. A favorite way of announcing this is to say, "Now would everyone please turn their phones to their most reverent setting, which is off."

Inviting

During this part of the rite, the clergy send out an invitation for the deities to join them and the other participants. The deities we call, especially the Mothers, are always present of course, but this process invites them to be with us in a more focused and aware state. It also opens a two-way conversation between them and the people who are honoring them.

Once everyone is lined up, but before you begin the procession, start the ritual by blowing three blasts on a conch trumpet, rattling a sistrum in three short bursts, or striking three blows on a hand drum. Don't use a metal gong or bell to begin the ritual unless Therasia is the only deity being honored in the rite.

Next, uncover the deity figurines and call to the gods and goddesses. The Mothers are always invited in first, even if other deities will be the focus of the rite.

> We invite Rhea, Therasia, Posidaeja, and [OTHER DEITY NAMES] to join us in this sacred rite.

Welcoming

Now the participants and clergy welcome each other as they also welcome the deities into the temple. Since this process is held and supported by mutual respect and connection, the welcome also extends to the temple itself as a being that participates in the ritual along with the human organizers and divine guests.

Move into the ritual space in an orderly procession while singing the opening chant:

> We enter the temple in love and peace;
> We enter the temple together.

Repeat the chant at least three times, until everyone is inside the ritual area.

Now the people who are carrying the deity figurines should set them on the altar one at a time. Again, the Mothers go first, followed by any other deities who will have a place on the altar. Set the trays and baskets on the side table.

Once the figurines are all on the altar, perform the call and response to honor the Mothers:

> Leader: We are children of the Earth.
> Participants: Hail, Rhea!
> Leader: We are children of the Sun.
> Participants: Hail, Therasia!
> Leader: We are children of the Sea.
> Participants: Hail, Posidaeja!

Welcome the Mothers and any other deities you'll be connecting with or honoring in this ritual:

> Welcome, Rhea! Welcome, Therasia! Welcome, Posidaeja!
> Welcome [OTHER DEITY NAMES]! The temple is consecrated by your presence.

Offering

A respectful relationship is about giving freely in a caring manner. This part of the ritual shows the divine that we don't want to take without first giving. The reciprocal nature of this free exchange, made with the consent of all concerned and without any coercion, is the key to establishing mutual trust between us and the deities we're asking for advice, assistance, or companionship. This is one of the ways we weave ourselves more deeply into the world around us so we can live fuller, more meaningful lives. Remember, the gods aren't cosmic vending machines. When we treat them like we would any honored guest or cherished elder, they show us an equal measure of generosity and respect.

First state the purpose of the ritual:

We have come here today to [CELEBRATE, ASK FOR HELP, GIVE THANKS, ETC.].

Make the offering:

Today we offer [OFFERING ITEM] to [DEITY].

For each offering item, retrieve it from the side table, dedicate it to the deity, then set it on the altar or pour the libation. Empty containers go back on the side table once you've given the offering. If there's more than one offering item, dedicate each one and set it on the altar or pour it out, then allow the clergy who's embodying the deity to respond before dedicating the next one. If it's appropriate to the focus of the ritual, the participants may sing or chant as each offering is made.

The clergy member who embodies each deity should respond to their offering immediately after it's made:

I have received your offering, and I thank you for it.

Clergy who embody the Mothers, including Ourania, may choose to say:

My children, I have received your offering, and I thank you for it.

Listening

Once the gifts we have to share have been freely given, it's our turn to receive. We've spent the previous stages of the ritual providing a welcoming and safe temple experience for each other and for the deities we've invited to attend. Now it's our turn to receive the gifts, blessings, counsel, or other experiences the deities wish to share with us. This involves listening rather than talking, if you see what I mean.

At this point in the ritual, the clergy who are embodying the deities move to the altar and speak. They might tell the story of what happens at this time of year in the sacred calendar or deliver a message to the participants. This can be scripted or extemporaneous, as the clergy desire. For more elaborate rituals, a mystery play could be performed, with multiple clergy acting out a story from the mythos. This portion of the ritual can involve interaction between the clergy and the participants, if appropriate. If one or more of the clergy are practicing trance possession, this is the time for that activity to take place, with the goal of delivering the deity's message to the participants. Remember that trance possession should be performed only by those with experience. It's absolutely NOT necessary to do trance possession to have a fulfilling ritual.

The altar and this ritual format connect the participants with the whole MMP pantheon, not just the ones you've officially called on. So always be respectful to all of them, since they'll be aware when you're doing ritual, even if you haven't invited them (in other words, don't joke or make offhand comments about deities who aren't a formal part of the ritual or you'll have to deal with their reaction sooner rather than later). You should also note that sometimes, a deity you haven't formally called to might "pop in" as you're doing ritual. This might happen because they sensed that they could help or support you in some way. Be open to hearing what they have to share with you, since it's liable to be perceptive and helpful.

After the message, story, or play is completed, the clergy move back from the altar and the participants spend a short time in silent meditation, focusing on the altar and contemplating what they've just experienced. No one should discuss their experiences until after the ritual is completed and the altar and other items have been disassembled and stored. The end of the silent meditation can be marked by a quiet drumbeat or the gentle rattling of a sistrum.

Returning

In this part of the ritual, participants give thanks to the deities for the message or experience that was shared with them during the Listening. After giving thanks, the people retrieve the deity figurines from the altar. Then participants and clergy leave the ritual space to carry the gifts of the temple out into the world as they return to their daily lives.

This portion of the ritual begins with a call and response:

Leader: We thank the Earth-Mother.
Participants: Hail, Rhea!
Leader: We thank the Sun-Mother.
Participants: Hail, Therasia!
Leader: We thank the Sea-Mother.
Participants: Hail, Posidaeja!

One of the clergy members then offers thanks:

We thank the Mothers! We thank [OTHER DEITY NAMES]!
Blessings upon you all, now and forever!

Each person who brought in a deity figurine now goes to the side table and picks up the basket or tray they used to bring the figurine into the ritual area. One at a time, each person takes the figurine they brought in from the altar and puts it back in their basket or tray. Do this in the opposite order the figurines were placed on the altar (in other words, with the Mothers removed last). Don't cover the deity figurines yet.

The clergy who embodied the deities, as well as any people who are carrying deity figurines, line up now in the same order they were in when they entered the ritual area. All the other participants line up behind them like they did in the procession that opened the ritual. The same person who led the opening chant now begins the closing chant. As everyone chants, the procession moves out of the ritual area in an orderly manner:

We carry the temple's blessings out into the world;
Peace be on us all, peace be on us all, peace be on us all.

Repeat the chant at least three times, no matter how long it takes you to leave the ritual area. Once everyone has left the ritual area, the rite is ended as it was begun, by three blasts of a conch trumpet, three short bursts on a sistrum, or three blows on a hand drum. Cover the deity figurines and set them someplace safe.

You may have moved out of the ritual area, but the ritual process isn't complete until the altar and any other accoutrements have been disassembled and properly stored, or prepared to be taken away, if they came from somewhere else. Until the ritual area has been fully disassembled, it's not appropriate to talk about any experiences you had during the rite. Allow the energy of the ritual to have its space. There will be plenty of time to talk about it after you're all done.

It's customary to share a meal after a group ritual; this is very much in keeping with the tradition of communal feasting that continued for centuries in Minoan Crete. The people who are in charge of the food can prepare the dining area and set out the food while the clergy and their helpers disassemble the ritual area. Obviously, this means the people in charge of the food should be different folx from the clergy who are running the ritual (many hands make light work). Once the temple has been appropriately disassembled or put to rest, everyone can gather to eat and discuss their experiences during the rite.

Solitary Ritual Format

Like group rituals, solitary rituals can be performed indoors or outdoors. If you've chosen an outdoor location, it's a good idea to have a sheltered area as an option in case of inclement weather.

Solitary rituals follow the same format as group rituals, with some modifications for the practicalities of having a single person completing all the steps by themselves. As with group rituals, solitary rituals should be completed reverently and with humility, though not somberly; joy is sacred, too. Ritual is a way to build your relationship with the divine, so bear that in mind throughout the preparation, performance, and cleanup phases. Simply doing ritual in this format, being your best and truest self, is a process that can bring blessings in and of itself.

Preparing

In this stage you're transforming a space that might have been used for other activities into a temple. You do this by "awakening" the space and the objects that will be used in the ritual, in other words, opening the location, the objects, and yourself to the presence of the divine. This applies equally to permanent altars and to temporary ritual spaces like public parks.

You can cleanse the ritual area and yourself by asperging with plain water, salt water, or herb water if you like. Gather your offerings near, but not on, the altar. Set up your altar, but without the deity figurine(s), which should be waiting covered, on trays or in shallow baskets, outside your ritual space. If you have more than one figurine, you can put them all on the same tray or in the same basket to make it easier to carry them. Now move outside the ritual space to begin.

If you're unable to move from an outer area to the ritual area, it's perfectly acceptable to begin a solitary ritual directly in front of the altar, with the deity figurines already placed on the altar but covered, as they would be in a basket or on a tray before the procession begins. But if you are able to complete the motion of the procession, please do so, since it's an important part of the ritual in terms of moving the energy and bringing the deities into the pace. In other words, don't use this as an excuse to skip the procession if you're reasonably able to do it. It's perfectly acceptable to complete the procession with the aid of crutches, a walker, a wheelchair, or any other assistive device—or even having someone carry you.

To perform the ritual if you're unable to do the procession, begin in front of the altar. Complete all the steps of Inviting and Welcoming, including the opening chant, from your place directly in front of the altar. It still counts as entering the temple, even if you're not physically moving during this part of the rite. Instead of bringing the deity figurines into the ritual area, simply lift them from the altar and set them back down. End the ritual in front of the altar, performing all the parts of Returning except for moving from the altar to another area.

Inviting

During this part of the rite, you send out an invitation for the deities to join you. Though the deities you call, especially the Mothers, are always present, this process invites them to be with you in a more focused and aware state and to open a two-way conversation between them and you.

Begin the ritual by blowing three blasts on a conch trumpet, playing three short bursts on a sistrum, or striking a hand drum three times. If you don't have any of these instruments, you can begin the ritual by clapping loudly three times. Don't use a metal gong or bell to begin the ritual unless Therasia is the only deity you're honoring in the rite.

Pick up the deity figurines, uncover them, and call to the divine. Always invite the Mothers first, regardless of whether other deities will be the focus of the rite.

> I invite Rhea, Therasia, Posidaeja, [OTHER DEITY NAMES]
> to join me in this sacred rite.

Welcoming

Now you welcome the deities into the temple. Since this process is held and supported by mutual respect and connection, the welcome also extends to the temple itself as a being that participates in the ritual along with you and your divine guests.

Still holding the deity figurines, move into the ritual space while you sing the opening chant:

> We enter the temple in love and peace;
> We enter the temple together.

Repeat the chant at least three times, no matter how long it takes you to enter the ritual area. You still use the word "together" in the chant, even if you're doing solitary ritual, because you're not really alone: the divine is with you. Repeat the chant until you're standing in front of the altar.

Place the deity figurine(s) on the altar, one at a time, beginning with the Mothers. Set your basket or tray on the side table. Say the following:

> I am a child of the Earth.
> Hail, Rhea!
> I am a child of the Sun.
> Hail, Therasia!
> I am a child of the Sea.
> Hail, Posidaeja!

Welcome the Mothers and any other deities you'll be connecting with or honoring in this ritual:

> Welcome, Rhea! Welcome, Therasia! Welcome, Posidaeja!
> Welcome [OTHER DEITY NAMES]! The temple is
> consecrated by your presence.

Offering

A respectful relationship is about giving freely in a caring manner. This part of the ritual shows the divine that you don't want to take without first giving. The reciprocal nature of this free exchange, made with the consent of all concerned and without any coercion, is the key to establishing mutual trust between you and the deities you're asking for advice, assistance, or companionship. This is one of the ways you weave yourself more deeply into the world around you so you can live a fuller, more meaningful life. Remember, the gods aren't cosmic vending machines. When you treat them like you would any honored guest or cherished elder, they show you an equal measure of generosity and respect.

State the purpose of the ritual:

> I have come here today to [CELEBRATE, ASK FOR HELP, GIVE THANKS, ETC.].

Make the offering:

> Today I offer [OFFERING ITEM] to [DEITY].

For each offering item, pick it up from the side table, dedicate it to the deity, then set it on the altar or pour the libation. Put any empty containers back on the side table. If there is more than one offering item, dedicate each one and set it on the altar or pour it out before dedicating the next one. If it's appropriate to the focus of the ritual, you can sing or chant as you make each offering. Take a moment to listen to your inner voice after making each offering and hear how each deity receives it before moving on to the next one.

Listening

Once the gifts you have to share have been freely given, it's your turn to receive. You've spent the previous stages of the ritual providing a welcoming and safe temple experience for the deities you've invited to attend. Now it's your turn to receive the gifts, blessings, counsel, or other experiences they wish to share with you.

You can choose to speak to the deities about the subject of your rite, or you can tell the story of what happens at this time of year in the sacred calendar. You can also perform a symbolic act that represents a sacred festival, like plucking grapes off the stem for the Feast of Grapes. Don't attempt trance possession during a solitary ritual. It's safest to undertake trance possession with at least one other experienced person present, and preferably in a larger group, since the purpose of trance possession is to allow the gods to speak through us to the community.

After you've completed the activity for this part of the rite, spend a short time in silent meditation, focusing on the altar and contemplating what you've just experienced. If you like, you can mark the end of this portion of the rite by a few soft drumbeats or the gentle rattling of a sistrum.

Returning

Now it's time to give thanks to the deities for the message or experience they shared with you during the Listening. After giving thanks, you'll retrieve the deity figurines from the altar. Then you'll leave the ritual space to carry the gifts of the temple out into the world as you return to your daily life.

Express your gratitude to the deities by saying the following:

I thank the Earth-Mother.
Hail, Rhea!
I thank the Sun-Mother.
Hail, Therasia!
I thank the Sea-Mother.
Hail, Posidaeja!

Continue with the following:

I thank the Mothers! I thank [OTHER DEITY NAMES]!
Blessings upon you all, now and forever!

Pick up your basket or tray from the side table and remove the deity figurines from the altar in the opposite order that you placed them there (in other words, removing the Mothers last). Carry the figurines out of the ritual area while singing the closing chant:

> We carry the temple's blessings out into the world;
> Peace be on us all, peace be on us all, peace be on us all.

Repeat the chant at least three times, no matter how long it takes you to leave the ritual area. Once you've left the ritual area, end the rite the way you began it, with three blasts of a conch trumpet, three short bursts on a sistrum, three blows on a hand drum, or three loud handclaps. Cover the deity figurines and set them someplace safe. Clean up your ritual area, putting away any objects that need to be stored. Avoid talking with anyone until you're finished taking down the ritual area.

It's a good idea to have something to eat and drink after a ritual, especially pure water. This helps you ground into the here and now. At your leisure, review your experiences during the ritual and contemplate what you can learn from them.

Ritual to Dedicate an Altar

The previous two ritual formats are our standard practice in MMP for groups and solitaries, but you'll want to customize them for different purposes, depending on the goal of the ritual. Customizing involves choosing which deity or deities to welcome, what to give as offerings, and what to include in the Listening portion of the rite. I've gone ahead and done that for you for this ritual and the next one. With these two rituals, you'll dedicate your altar to its purpose and begin a relationship with the Minoan deities. You can come back to these two rituals any time you want to set up a new altar or expand your connections with the pantheon.

Once you've set up your sacred space, you need to dedicate it to its use as a way to connect with the divine. If you're setting up a permanent altar, or at least a long-term one, you can dedicate it once at the beginning and not have to do it again. If you're going to set up your altar each time you use it and then take it down and store it away after you're done, dedicate it the first time you set it up. Then, if you feel it's necessary, you can asperge it any future time you set it up to "freshen up" the energy. You don't need to do a full re-dedication ritual unless something happens to it that makes you feel like it needs more than just an asperging (a large dog crashes into it, a pot of spaghetti is spilled onto it—something major).

An altar that will be set up just once, such as for a group ritual, doesn't need to be dedicated in a separate rite. Asperging it will be sufficient. Then the presence of the deities will consecrate it as needed for the purpose of the ritual. But for a home altar that's going to be the focus of your personal spiritual practice, begin your relationship with the altar by performing this rite of dedication. This sets it up as the connection point between you and the divine and lets the deities know they can meet you there. You can also dedicate individual items as you add them to your sacred space. This is especially appropriate for deity figurines. You'll want to dedicate them to the specific deities they represent.

Be sure to read through the standard ritual format for solitaries, above, before performing this rite. The description above includes information about the meaning of each section of the ritual. It's important that you understand the "why" as much as the "how" for the six parts of the ritual format. I've left those explanations out of this and the next ritual to save space and avoid repetition.

Though many modern Pagans like to use incense or herb bundles to consecrate altars and sacred space, in MMP we use incense as an offering. While it does have a sacred aspect, incense is a gift to the gods. Our experience with the deities of our pantheon tells us that they prefer incense to be used as an offering and not as a method to sacralize any given area. So how can we dedicate our altars? What did the Minoans do?

The Minoans asperged their ritual areas, people, livestock, and anything else they wanted to bless, dedicate, or consecrate. Asperging is a fancy word that simply means sprinkling a liquid. It's one of the oldest methods of blessing and consecration. The simplest way is to dip your fingers in the liquid and flick the drops over the area or object (or person). You could also use a tool like a paintbrush, a stalk of wheat or barley, or a bundle of herbs—dip the business end in the liquid and sprinkle a few drops as a blessing. A brush or other instrument that's made specifically for the purpose of consecrating by sprinkling a liquid is called an aspergillum. These are pictured on several Minoan seals.

What kind of liquid should you use? Water that's been blessed for a sacred purpose is the most common choice around the world and throughout time. I'm especially fond of water that I've gathered from meaningful sources: sacred wells, lakes, rivers, streams, springs, the ocean. Bottled spring water is a good choice if you don't have ready access to a natural body of water. If you like, you can set the water out in the sunlight or moonlight to charge it, ask a deity to bless it, or drop a favorite stone into it before using it to asperge your altar. Water is the basis of life on this planet. Its very presence evokes the powers of nature.

Certain herbs that the Minoans were familiar with have long been used for energetic cleansing. Among these are rue, wormwood, and sage (European garden sage, a.k.a. *Salvia officinalis*, not North American white sage). You can steep one of these herbs in some water in the same way you would make herb tea, then use the resulting infusion to asperge your sacred space. It's likely that the ancient Minoans saved the blood from their animal sacrifices and added it to wine for asperging fields and livestock, and possibly even for blessing people. I don't recommend that for modern use, though!

To dedicate and sacralize your altar using a liquid, first put it in a container that's wide enough that you can dip your fingers or your asperging tool into it easily. Simply dip your fingers or your chosen tool into the liquid and flick a few drops of it onto your altar at the appropriate time during the ritual. You don't need to hit every item on your altar with a drop of the liquid. What you're doing here is essentially wafting the energy of the liquid over your sacred space with the gesture of your hand or tool. Do be careful that you don't get any of your altar ware too wet.

So go ahead and set up your sacred space, prepare your asperging liquid, and we'll get started.

The Ritual

Preparing

You'll begin this ritual with your altar set up but without any deity figurines on it. Instead, prepare the deity figurines by setting them in a basket or on a tray and covering them with a soft cloth or basket lid. Set the basket or tray outside the ritual area, away from your altar. Your offering for this ritual should be incense in a scent or blend that you associate with sacred space and "clean" energy. Gather your incense, a fireproof incense holder, a charcoal block if you'll need one, matches or a lighter, your asperging liquid, and an aspergillum if you're using one, on the side table.

Take a few deep breaths and bring your focus—your awareness of your body, your thoughts, your emotions—down to the ritual area. When you're ready, begin the Inviting.

Inviting

Begin the ritual by blowing three blasts on a conch trumpet, playing three short bursts on a sistrum, or striking a hand drum three times. If you don't have any of these instruments, you can begin the ritual by clapping loudly three times.

Pick up the deity figurines, uncover them, and call to the divine. For this rite, you'll call on just the Mothers by name, regardless of how many deity figurines you're carrying in. As the heads of the pantheon, the Mothers are the Powers that consecrate your altar. They are the core of the pantheon and they connect you with all the other deities.

I invite Rhea, Therasia, and Posidaeja to join me in this sacred rite.

Welcoming

Still holding the deity figurines, move into the ritual space while singing the opening chant:

> We enter the temple in love and peace;
> We enter the temple together.

Repeat the chant at least three times, until you're in front of the altar.

Place the deity figurine(s) on the altar, one at a time, beginning with the Mothers. Set your basket or tray on the side table.

Now say the following:

> I am a child of the Earth.
> Hail, Rhea!
> I am a child of the Sun.
> Hail, Therasia!
> I am a child of the Sea.
> Hail, Posidaeja!

Welcome the Mothers:

> Welcome, Rhea! Welcome, Therasia! Welcome, Posidaeja!
> The temple is consecrated by your presence.

Offering

State the purpose of the ritual:

> I have come here today to dedicate this altar to its purpose as a point of connection between myself and the Minoan deities.

Make the offering:

> Today I offer incense to the Mothers.

Set the incense on the altar and light it. Wait until the smoke curls up, then take a moment to listen to your inner voice to make sure the Mothers have accepted the offering.

Listening

Pick up the water and the aspergillum, if you're using one. Position yourself in front of the altar. Draw in a few slow, deep breaths to center yourself. Now call to the Mothers:

> I ask the Mothers to bless this altar. I dedicate it to the deities of Modern Minoan Paganism. I ask that this altar become a point of connection between myself and the divine.

Now sprinkle the water over the altar, using your fingers or the aspergillum, whichever you have chosen. This act dedicates your altar and awakens it as a point of connection between you and the deities of our pantheon. When you're done asperging the altar, set the water and the aspergillum aside.

After you've completed this part of the rite, spend a short time in silent meditation, focusing on the altar and contemplating what you've just experienced. Listen for any messages the Mothers or other deities might have for you. If you like, you can mark the end of this portion of the rite by a few soft drumbeats or the gentle rattling of a sistrum.

Returning

Express your gratitude to the deities by saying the following:

> I thank the Earth-Mother.
> Hail, Rhea!
> I thank the Sun-Mother.
> Hail, Therasia!
> I thank the Sea-Mother.
> Hail, Posidaeja!

Continue with the following:

I thank the Mothers! Blessings upon you all, now and forever!

Pick up your basket or tray from the side table and remove the deity figurines from the altar in the opposite order that you placed them there (in other words, removing the Mothers last). Carry the figurines out of the ritual area while singing the closing chant:

We carry the temple's blessings out into the world;
Peace be on us all, peace be on us all, peace be on us all.

Repeat the chant at least three times. Once you've left the ritual area, end the rite the way you began it, with three blasts of a conch trumpet, three short bursts on a sistrum, three blows on a hand drum, or three loud handclaps. Cover the deity figurines and set them someplace safe. Clean up your ritual area, putting away any objects that need to be stored.

It's a good idea to have something to eat and drink after a ritual, especially pure water. This helps you ground into the here and now. At your leisure, review your experiences during the ritual and contemplate what you can learn from them.

Your sacred space is now ready to be used for meditation, rituals, and other sacred activities. You can asperge it briefly before use if you feel it needs "freshening up," but it's not usually necessary to perform the dedication rite again.

Ritual to Connect with the Minoan Pantheon

Maybe you don't know which deity or deities you'd like to form relationships with. Or maybe you already have relationships with one or two, but would like to strengthen your connection with the Minoan pantheon. Whether you're just starting out or an old hat, this ritual is a good choice for developing or firming up your rapport with the gods and goddesses of our pantheon.

This ritual formally introduces you to the Mothers, letting them know that you're present and ready to learn from them and, through them, from the other deities. The Mothers are where it all starts: the pantheon, yes, but also creation (at least in a symbolic way). So start with this ritual, then you can move onto meeting and developing relationships with other deities.

One of the hardest things to do in spiritual practice is to be open to whatever comes and accept it for what it is. This ritual will be more effective if you can allow yourself to receive whatever thoughts and feelings might come to you without judging them. Do your best to be receptive to whatever comes to you and allow yourself to be open to new ideas and experiences.

For the best results, perform this ritual with an altar or shrine that's already been dedicated. That will make it easier to focus and draw in the Mothers' energy. You can add other deities to your altar later without re-dedicating it. Or you can set up a new altar to another god or goddess when you're ready. But start here, since the Mothers are the entryway into the pantheon.

Be sure to read through the standard ritual format for solitaries, above, before performing this rite. The description above includes information about the meaning of each section of the ritual. It's important that you understand the "why" as much as the "how" for the six parts of the ritual format. I've left those explanations out of this ritual to save space and avoid repetition.

It's a good idea to use a candle or oil lamp for this ritual. The flame is a helpful focus for the meditation, making it easier to receive whatever the gods have to tell or show you. Set it in a fireproof holder in a safe and sturdy spot on the altar so you don't have to worry about it tipping over. Arrange a place where you can sit in front of the altar and be able to see the lit candle or oil lamp clearly. This can be in a chair or on the floor, however you're comfortable. You'll need to sit for several minutes during the central part of the ritual.

It's especially important for this ritual that you be relaxed so you can sense whatever messages might be waiting for you. So be sure you have plenty of time—it's never a good idea to rush a ritual—and also be sure you won't be disturbed. Double-check that your phone is turned off, your pets are taken care of, and any people you live with know to give you some quiet time.

An appropriate offering for this ritual involves the number three in one way or another, since you're focusing on the Mothers here. You could do a triple libation with wine (Rhea), water (Posidaeja), and honey (Therasia). Or you could offer three sticks of incense in different scents or three flowers in different colors. Three pieces of homemade bread would also work.

You'll be receiving a lot of new information in this ritual. You might want to have a pen and paper handy to write it down afterward, but don't include that as part of the ritual. Let the ritual be its own separate, sacred act. Then feel free to jot down notes after you're done, both for reflection and to make sure you don't forget anything. Now let's begin.

The Ritual
Preparing
You'll begin this ritual with your altar set up but without any deity figurines on it. Instead, prepare deity figurines of the three Mothers by setting them in a basket or on a tray and covering them with a soft cloth or basket lid. Set the basket or tray outside the ritual area, away from your altar. Gather your offering items on the side table. Make sure the altar includes an oil lamp or candle and you have matches or a lighter on the side table.

Take a few deep breaths and bring your focus—your awareness of your body, your thoughts, your emotions—down to the ritual area. When you're ready, begin the Inviting.

Inviting
Begin the ritual by blowing three blasts on a conch trumpet, playing three short bursts on a sistrum, or striking a hand drum three times. If you don't have any of these instruments, you can begin the ritual by clapping your hands loudly three times.

Pick up the deity figurines, uncover them, and call to the Mothers.

I invite Rhea, Therasia, and Posidaeja to join me in this
sacred rite.

Welcoming

Still holding the deity figurines, move into the ritual space while
singing the opening chant:

> We enter the temple in love and peace;
> We enter the temple together.

Repeat the chant at least three times. Place the deity figurines
on the altar one at a time. Set your basket or tray on the side table.
Say the following:

> I am a child of the Earth.
> Hail, Rhea!
> I am a child of the Sun.
> Hail, Therasia!
> I am a child of the Sea.
> Hail, Posidaeja!

Welcome the Mothers :

> Welcome, Rhea! Welcome, Therasia! Welcome, Posidaeja!
> The temple is consecrated by your presence.

Offering

State the purpose of the ritual:

> I have come here today to present myself to the Mothers
> and to learn from them.

Make the offering:

> Today I offer [OFFERING ITEMS] to the Mothers.

For each offering item, dedicate it to the deity, then set it on
the altar or pour the libation into a container on the altar. Take a

moment to listen to your inner voice after making each offering and hear how each deity receives it.

Listening

Light the candle or oil lamp on the altar. Take a seat in front of the altar, positioning yourself so you can see the flame clearly. Draw in a few slow, deep breaths to center yourself. Now call to the Mothers:

> Great Mothers, I am here before you. I am ready to connect with you. I am ready to learn whatever you have to teach me.

Now focus on the flame and *listen*. For many of us, this is the hardest part. You don't have to completely empty your mind, but you do need to focus on your intuition, that inner voice that tells you what's really going on. It's through this inner voice that the gods speak to us, and through our hearts as well. You might experience certain thoughts, ideas, or images—or you might feel a wave of emotion. Often, with the presence of the Mothers, we find ourselves feeling a kind of comfort and warmth that we haven't felt since we were children. Allow yourself to experience whatever comes to you, whether it's thoughts or feelings or both, without judgment. It is what it is. Let the experience flow until you feel it's done. Don't rush it, but eventually you'll know that it's over.

After you've completed this part of the rite, spend a short time in silent meditation, focusing on the altar and contemplating what you've just experienced. If you like, you can mark the end of this portion of the rite with a few soft drumbeats or the gentle rattling of a sistrum.

Returning

Express your gratitude to the Mothers by saying the following:

I thank the Earth-Mother.
Hail, Rhea!
I thank the Sun-Mother.
Hail, Therasia!
I thank the Sea-Mother.
Hail, Posidaeja!

Continue with the following:

I thank the Mothers! Blessings upon you all, now and
forever!

Pick up your basket or tray from the side table and remove the
deity figurines from the altar in the opposite order that you placed
them there. Carry the figurines out of the ritual area while singing
the closing chant:

We carry the temple's blessings out into the world;
Peace be on us all, peace be on us all, peace be on us all.

Repeat the chant at least three times. Once you've left the
ritual area, end the rite the way you began it, with three blasts of a
conch trumpet, three short bursts on a sistrum, three blows on a
hand drum, or three loud handclaps. Cover the deity figurines
and set them someplace safe. Clean up your ritual area, putting
away any objects that need to be stored.

It's a good idea to have something to eat and drink after a
ritual, especially pure water. This helps you ground into the here
and now. At your leisure, review your experiences during the
ritual and contemplate what you can learn from them. Now that
the ritual is over, you can pick up that pen and paper and write
down anything you feel is important to remember.

Making Offerings

Just like we might offer a beloved guest something to eat or drink or share the batch of cookies we just baked with Grandma when she comes to visit, most Pagans make offerings to their gods and goddesses. Sometimes people who are unfamiliar with Paganism mistake offerings for a sort of 'cosmic vending machine'—put in an offering and out pops a blessing. But the gods aren't vending machines and personally, if my friends and family only did nice things for me when they wanted something from me, I'd get annoyed. I'm sure they'd be pretty upset if I treated them that way, too. That's not how the system works. We have relationships with the gods just like we have relationships with people. We give to each other out of love and caring, and we should give to the gods the same way. *Freely given or not at all*, as my first priestess used to say.

Thinking about what kind of meaning you're trying to convey to the gods with your offering can help you decide what to give: bread to give thanks for the harvest, flowers to celebrate a happy occasion, and so on. Also consider the location. If you're going to put an offering on your altar, it needs to be small enough to fit. If you're leaving an offering outdoors, make sure it's inert (like a stone) or biodegradable (like food or flowers) and won't be poisonous to any wildlife that might take a taste.

We make offerings to thank the gods and goddesses for being in our lives, for blessing us, and for making our world richer and more meaningful. Offerings help keep us in relationship with the gods so that when we do need their help, they know who we are, have a connection with us, and will be more likely to come to our aid. This is an activity that goes back to Neolithic times, if not earlier. Let's look at the kinds of offerings the Minoans made and see how we can use or adapt them for Modern Minoan Paganism.

Making the Offering

Offerings to the deities are a standard part of our spiritual practice, whether the offering is food or a libation or incense or something else entirely. As I mentioned above, offerings should be inert (a stone, a seashell) or biodegradable (incense, food, drink, flowers, and so on). You should choose your offering based on the deity you're honoring and the goal or focus of your ritual. Each god or goddess has offerings we've found them to prefer, and some have offerings they don't care for. They're all listed in Chapter 3.

On a more general level, there are some offering items that we've found to provoke strong reactions from the Minoan deities, so you should seriously consider not including them in your practice. High up on this list is meat. Yes, the Minoans ate meat, and lots of it, but the deities' reaction to it is very unpredictable. I've known people who hunted who offered a portion of their venison kill to the Minelathos or Britomartis and had it accepted, but I would still check first to be sure before making that offering. Offering meat that you've purchased is a very iffy thing, so tread carefully, even if you're simply trying to share one of your favorite foods with the gods. They have taste preferences every bit as much as we do, and their reasons for refusal won't always be obvious from a human point of view.

Another risky offering item is blood. Blood of any sort (venous blood, menstrual blood, birthing blood, the blood from an animal you've hunted or slaughtered) has powerful connotations. Its presence in a sacred setting can easily offend or anger any number of deities. Offering your own blood can also tie you to the deity in ways you may not understand or intend. Be especially careful when offering blood of any sort to Underworld deities unless that's where you want to end up.

If you feel compelled to offer blood of any sort, please take the time to connect with the god or goddess and make sure you understand the implications of what you're doing. The gods' reactions will tend to differ from one worshiper to another, so you can't necessarily depend on someone else's experience here. We know the ancient Minoans collected and used the blood of sacrificed animals in some way, but there were doubtless strong rules and taboos associated with the practice. Quite a few people have shared visions of private/secret women's rituals involving menstrual blood, but we aren't sure exactly what was involved or what the protocol was. The same issues apply for sexual fluids, regardless of your physical sex or gender. Since we don't know for certain how the Minoans used these substance ritually and what methods they used to safeguard themselves in the process, it's best to tread very carefully and avoid unnecessary experimentation. There is no one-size-fits-all answer for this one.

If you'd like to make an offering but you're not sure the deity will accept the item you've chosen, you can do a "test run" before your ritual just to make sure. Place the offering on the side table near your altar. Take a few moments to clear your mind, then call to the deity to let them know you're considering making this specific offering. Then listen. You won't necessarily hear words, but you'll probably get a feeling, a sense of either acceptance or rejection of whatever you'd like to offer. On rare occasions, rejection can be dramatic, like with cups tipping over and spilling or objects falling off the table. But usually, unless you've decided to offer something really strange, you'll get the sense that it's all right to go ahead.

Making an offering is a part of the MMP standard ritual format, but you don't have to perform a full ritual to make an offering. If you have an altar already set up, you can simply place the offering on the altar (or pour it into a bowl on the altar, if it's a libation) along with a few words letting the deity know what you're doing and why. Don't just toss the item on the altar and walk away. That's rude. Quiet your mind and focus your thoughts, address the god or goddess politely, make the offering, then take a few moments to listen. You're listening to make sure the item was accepted and to find out whether the deity has anything else to say to you. If you like, you can make the Minoan salute as well, as a gesture of respect.

Normally, you should dispose of offerings as soon as your ritual is over and the altar is being disassembled. If you make offerings on an active altar that will be left standing after the ritual is over, you can leave them there overnight or longer. How long they remain there will depend on the nature and goals of your ritual and any messages the deities give you. Never leave food or other organic material sitting on an altar long enough to rot. MMP doesn't normally practice reversion of offerings. Once an item has been given, it belongs to the gods and may not be taken back by humans.

Please dispose of all offering materials responsibly. Don't litter or endanger wildlife. Food items, flowers, and similar offerings can go in the compost or be buried. Liquids can be poured onto the ground (the soil, please, not a paved surface). Avoid placing offering items in the garbage if at all possible.

Consumable Offerings

Like most people in the ancient world, the Minoans put offerings on their altars and shrines on a regular basis. They had special offering stands that looked like terracotta versions of modern footed cake plates or little three-legged stools. They also used ordinary dishes—plates, bowls, and cups—for their offerings. They would choose a container that was appropriate for the offering and that would fit on their altar or shrine shelf, much like many modern Pagans do. They also left offerings outdoors at tombs, cave shrines, and peak sanctuaries and probably at other outdoor sites as well. In these cases they usually just set out the offering item without any kind of dish or container.

To make an offering at their home shrine, the Minoans might set out some fruit or flowers or a little bit of whatever they were having for dinner, particularly if it was a special-occasion meal. Bread was a very popular offering throughout the ancient world. If you feel inspired to do a little baking, homemade bread makes for a special gift to the gods. If you have a flower garden or some potted plants, a bloom or two that you've grown yourself also makes for an eloquent and beautiful offering, but fresh flowers from your local shop will work just fine, too.

Incense has been a popular offering for millennia. Burning some incense is a great way to perfume your sacred space and show the gods that you're paying attention to them. I like to set aside certain types or scents of incense for individual deities so they know they're getting something special that I don't offer to anyone else. If a particular type of incense makes you automatically think of a specific god or goddess whenever you smell it, it's a good one to offer to that deity.

When you're making an offering, don't just toss the item down and walk away. If somebody did that to me, I'd probably be offended, so I expect the gods would be, too. Take a few moments to turn it into a little ritual. Slow down, take a few deep breaths, and focus on what you're doing. Think about who you're making the offering to: a specific god or goddess, a nature spirit, the whole pantheon. Focus on the recipient, call their name, and tell them why you're making the offering. Set your offering out (or light your incense) in a mindful way. Then take a few more moments to wait quietly until you feel the offering has been received. Then you can step away and do other things.

The question of how long to leave a consumable offering out is really a personal one. For something like incense, once it has burned down, you can clean up the ash and consider it done. If your offering includes food or flowers, you can leave it out overnight if you like. This gives the energy of your gift some time to be 'digested' by those you're giving it to. You might feel you need to leave it longer than just overnight. Listen to your inner voice in these matters. A vase of fresh flowers could easily last a week if you change the water regularly, but a dish of cooked food will probably become unpleasant after a day or two. Use both your intuition and your common sense to determine how long to leave it. The gods don't want wilted flowers or spoiled food any more than you do.

If your offering included food, it's not acceptable to eat the food yourself, even if it's still in good condition. That's the equivalent of taking back the gift. You should dispose of it in a way that feels right to you, whether that's adding it to your compost pile or setting it outdoors for the wild animals to share, provided it's safe for them to eat. Avoid putting offerings in the trash if at all possible.

Poured Offerings

The libation may have been the most common kind of offering in ancient Crete. A libation is simply the pouring out of a liquid onto the ground or into a special container. This is different from simply setting out a cup of whatever you're offering. The act of pouring is a little ritual in itself, and the liquid spilling out of the cup shows that you're giving it away and won't be drinking it yourself later on.

You can perform a libation with pretty much any kind of liquid you'd be willing to drink. We know the Minoans used wine and milk, and they may have used water as well. If you associate a particular herb with the god or goddess you're giving the libation to, you could steep that herb in the liquid of your choice. The Minoans added herbs to both wine and milk to flavor them. Or you could brew up a cup of herb tea and offer that.

If you don't drink wine but would like to make a libation to Dionysus, I've found that he enjoys dark purple grape juice as well (but not the clear/white kind). However, if you do drink wine and choose to offer him grape juice instead, be aware that he's liable to feel cheated and be unhappy with your offering. It's always a good idea to think about what would count as good manners if you were entertaining friends and wanted to offer them a drink. If you had a glass of wine in your hand but you offered them grape juice, how would they feel?

The Minoans produced a wide variety of rhytons (pitchers) that they used for libations. A lot of them have really imaginative designs: cattle where the liquid pours out the mouth; female figures where the liquid pours out the breasts or from a jar the woman is holding; bird-shaped jugs where the liquid pours out the beak. I suspect they also made libations from their drinking cups as well. So you could choose pretty much any kind of pitcher, cup, or glass to make your libations with. I'm especially fond of the white porcelain cow-shaped cream pitchers that are available in cooking supply shops. They remind me of the Minoan cow-shaped rhytons.

In terms of how you make your libation, first you need to decide whether you're going to do it indoors or outdoors. If you make your offering outdoors, it's a simple matter of choosing a spot and pouring it out on the ground (the actual Earth, please, and not a paved surface). You could dig a hole if you like. Sometimes I do that when I'm making an offering to the ancestors, since pouring the drink into a hole makes me think of it going down to the Underworld. That's a similar idea to the little moats the Minoans built into the floor around the bases of the pillars in the cellars of their temples.

Indoors, obviously you need a container to pour the liquid into. The container should go on the altar so you're pouring the libation onto the altar in the same way that you would set a solid offering on the altar. A bowl that's bigger than the amount of liquid you're going to offer is a good choice. You want it large enough to catch any splashes as you pour, unless you just happen to like wine stains on your altar cloth.

When you make the libation, take your time. Stop and think about what you're doing. Take a few deep breaths. If you're not making the offering as part of a full ritual, name the deity you're making the offering to and tell them why, whether it's for a particular occasion or just to say 'thank you' in general. Then pour your liquid slowly. Watch the stream of liquid as it twists and turns on its way down. Feel the energy of your offering pouring out to the gods in gratitude and celebration. When you're done, take a few moments to let the energy settle before moving on to anything else.

If you've done your libation outdoors, there's nothing to dispose of. But if you've made your offering indoors, you'll need to decide how to deal with the remains. Once the liquid has been poured, the offering is made, so it doesn't need to sit out overnight unless you just feel that need. Even if I've made the libation indoors, I like to dispose of the liquid in my garden or at least in a potted plant if I can. But pouring it down the drain is acceptable if there's no outdoor option. For all we know, the

Minoans did just that—after all, they had enclosed sewer systems in their towns.

Other Kinds of Offerings

In addition to tangible items like food, drink, incense, and flowers, people sometimes like to make offerings of intangibles: their time and effort, for instance. These aren't objects that can be set on an altar. Instead, they're transformational gifts to the gods. What on Earth am I talking about?

You might be developing a relationship with Rhea, who's an Mother Earth figure, and in the course of that process you might feel like making her an offering of something more profound than just a bowl of fruit or some incense. Maybe you decide to get a bunch of people together and go clean up your local park or beach, and you decide to make that whole project—all your time and labor and energy—into an offering to her.

Maybe you write a poem or a story or a song as an offering to a deity. You could choose to share it just with the deity, or give it away for free, or sell it and donate the proceeds to a charity that's in alignment with the deity's energy and direction.

Some people like to make pilgrimages to sacred sites or to special places in nature as an offering to the gods. Some people enjoy organizing community events, dedicating their time and labor as an offering. Some people do good works—volunteering at a soup kitchen or shelter, taking food to homeless people, helping out anyone who needs a hand—specifically as offerings to their gods and goddesses. Suggestions for offerings of this type are included in the listings in Chapter 3.

When you're making this kind of offering, it's helpful to include a ritual before and after to sort of 'make it official.' In this case, you would use the standard ritual format, but during the Offering portion of the rite, instead of setting something on the altar, you would announce your offering to the deity. Then during the Listening portion, meditate on the activity you intend to perform as an offering and pay attention to any response the deity has for you. Then go and do the project, whatever it is. Soon after you're finished, go to your altar again and perform the standard ritual format. During the Offering section, tell the gods you've completed the project, reminding them what it was and why you did it. Then during the Listening part of the ritual, meditate on their response to your offering.

Practically anything you can do can become an offering if that's your intention. This is a great way to bring the sacred into a larger part of your life. It's also a wonderful way to show your dedication to your favorite deities.

Ecstatic Postures

The practice of assuming a specific pose and holding it while going into trance goes back millennia in many different cultures around the world, but it's a method that isn't very well known in modern times. These poses are called ecstatic postures. We can find them in art going back to the Paleolithic. As you might expect, they show up in Minoan art as well. Ecstatic postures are used for healing, spirit journeys, connecting with deities, and showing respect for the divine.

One major source of ecstatic postures in Minoan art is the vast number of votive (offering) figurines that have been found in the cave shrines and at the peak sanctuaries on Crete. Many of these figurines show the worshiper making a gesture called the 'Minoan salute': the right hand is loosely curled into a fist and the back of the hand is placed against the forehead. The left arm hangs at the side in a relaxed position. The Minoan salute also appears on seals and seal impressions from Minoan archaeological sites.

We use the Minoan salute in MMP to show respect for the divine, both during formal ritual and in more casual situations like the beginning of a meditation. Simply holding the position for a minute or two while focusing your thoughts on a particular god or goddess is a great way to create a connection with that deity. We also use this pose to salute the Sun, the Moon, the stars, and natural features like lakes, rivers, and mountains. The divine is everywhere around us. Acknowledging that as we're out and about adds another dimension to our spiritual practice.

Fig. 17: Bronze figurine, Minoan salute, Knossos

Another pose we use in MMP is the Upraised Arms position. This posture appears on a number of bell jar figurines. They're called that because the skirt part of the figurine was thrown on a potter's wheel and is shaped like a jar. The upper bodies of the figurines were hand-formed to make delightful faces and interesting headdresses full of sacred symbolism.

Fig. 18: Bell jar goddess figurines, Crete

While the Minoan salute is used by worshipers, both in and out of ritual, the Upraised Arms pose is used by priestesses who are drawing down a goddess for ritual. With the arms up and the palms facing in toward the body, the pose makes it so a goddess can slip down onto the priestess for ritual, almost like putting on a comfortable garment. This pose can be used for any of the goddesses in the Modern Minoan pantheon, though it's recommended that only experienced clergy use it to draw down Ourania, since her presence can be especially disorienting.

For more information about ecstatic postures—how to use them safely and how to explore new ones you find in ancient art—please consult the book *Ecstatic Body Postures*, listed in the Resources section at the end of this book. You should be aware, however, that the Realm of the Dead posture is incorrect as described in *Ecstatic Body Postures*. The Cycladic figurines on which this posture is based are displayed standing upright in museums, but they were originally found lying down in tombs. If you want to use the Realm of the Dead posture, for the best safety and efficacy, do it lying down. In MMP we associate this posture with Ariadne, whose mythological cycle involves going down to the Underworld every year to care for the spirits of the dead and then returning to the World Above.

Chapter 6:
Devotionals

One really simple, meaningful way to connect with the divine is the devotional. This is a simple set of words—a prayer, really—that helps you focus on that deity's energy. A devotional can be done anywhere: in front of your altar, during a break at work or school, when you're out for a walk in nature. All you need is the words and a few moments of mindful attention. Read them slowly out loud, allowing each word to find its way out into the world and inward, into your understanding.

If you use a devotional regularly, you'll find that you end up memorizing it without really trying. That's fine, but don't allow it to become rote, something that you rattle off as a habit without focusing on it. Every time you say it, continue to pay attention. Allow the words to shape a meaning for you, then let that meaning connect you with the divine in real time.

I often like to combine a devotional with a small offering—a stick of incense or a flower, for instance. You don't have to do a full ritual for something like that. For me, devotionals are a great way to start or end the day. Performing a devotional first thing in the morning sets the tone for the day and helps me remember that everything I do is sacred in one way or another. When I do a devotional to a god or goddess in the morning, I find my thoughts turning back to them throughout the day, which is a great way to gently build a relationship with them and discover how they're relevant to our modern lives. Performing a devotional when you get home from work is a good way to 'reset' yourself, shake off the mundane, and find your footing in the sacred again. And doing a devotional at bedtime can make for awesome dreams.

If you come from a formal spiritual tradition of any sort, you might be used to adding some sort of official ending to devotionals and prayers, such as the 'Amen' of Christianity or the 'So mote it be' of Wicca. If you already have a word or phrase you're comfortable with, then go ahead and use it. I like to end many of my prayers and devotionals with this phrase: 'So it is and so we let it be.' Another possibility that I use regularly is a benediction that Emily Dickinson wrote because she didn't like the Christian "Father, Son, and Holy Ghost" one that she grew up with. I find it appropriate for Minoan spirituality because of the bee and butterfly symbolism in Minoan sacred art:

In the name of the bee,
And of the butterfly,
And of the breeze, amen.

Of course, you don't have to add anything at the end if you don't want to. But sometimes it's nice to have a little something that tells your brain you're done and it's time to move on to the next activity.

When you're first setting out on a spiritual path, it can be tempting to try to do everything all at once so you don't miss out on anything. But it's not possible to keep up that kind of tempo for long, and you'll only end up disappointed sooner or later. It's best to choose just one or two deities to connect with, at least to start, and focus on them for a while. Don't try to do devotionals to all, or even most, of the gods and goddesses. Begin with the ritual to connect with the Mothers in the previous chapter, then slowly branch out from there. Choose one or two deities who call to you the most and give them your attention, deepen your relationship with them for a while. Then move on from there, one step at a time.

Rhea

Holy Mother Earth,
Rhea the All-Giver,
Help me to remember that I am a part
Of the Earth beneath my feet,
The life around me and above me.
May I walk each day
Knowing in my heart
That every grain of soil,
Every drop of water,
Every breath of air,
Every beat of my heart
Is holy.

Fig. 19: Seal impression of goddess on mountain, Knossos

Fig. 20: Goddess with Griffin fresco, Akrotiri

Therasia

Fire of Heaven,
Sun-Mother,
Shine your radiance upon me.
As your power moves my spirit,
So your brilliance fills my heart
And warms me to my core.
Help me to stay seated in
The strength and passion
That is your gift to us
And to remember
That your light shines within me, always.

Posidaeja

Grandmother Ocean
I call to you
As you embrace the whole world
With your gentle ebb and flow.
Help me to roll with the changing tide
And feel the depths of the ancient sea
Within me.
Water of Life,
Show me the way
To swim gently through my days,
And let your softly lapping waves
Send me sweet sleep through my nights.

Fig. 21: Marine ware jug, Palaikastro

Fig. 22: Seal ring, goddess rising up from the Earth, Thisbe

Ariadne

Sweet Ariadne of the Mysteries,
I ask that you guide me
Along the Labyrinth of life,
The twisting and turning path
That winds out into the world
And coils deep inside me.
Take me safely to the deepest, darkest places
And bring me surely back out again
So that I may be a beacon of hope
For those who have not made the journey yet,
So we may all find the Mystery
That lies within.

Arachne

Spinner-Woman,
Fate-Weaver,
In whose web
We are all tangled,
Grant that the twist of my life
May wind strong and sure
To its very end.
Help me to remember
That the quivering of the thread
Is my connection
To all living
But most especially
To you.

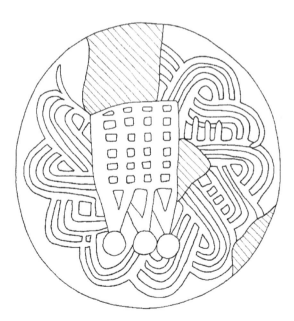

Fig. 23: Seal with loom weights and interwoven threads, Hagia Triada

Fig. 24: Garland fresco, Knossos

Antheia

Star of the Sea,
Fair Blossom,
Beneath whose feet
Flowers spring up
With every step:
Help me to see
The beauty in the world
And to walk
With love and grace,
Remembering always
That the loveliness of life
Is shared freely
Among those
Whose hearts are open to it.

Tauros Asterion

Bull of Crete,
Starry One,
Who reaches from Heaven
To Earth,
Help me to remember
That I am both
Physical and transcendent,
That above and below
Are mirrors of each other
Within you
And within me.

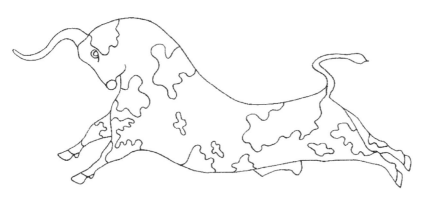

Fig. 25: Bull from Bull Leaper fresco, Knossos

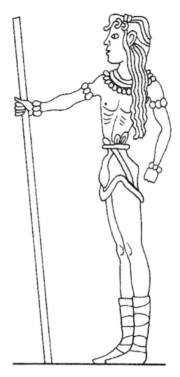

Fig. 26: Detail, Chieftain cup, Hagia Triada

Korydallos

Singing Lark,
Son of the Sun,
Your chiming laughter
Warms my heart.
Help me to find
The humor in life,
The joy and the playfulness
So I may dance the dance
As a child does,
With ease and delight.

Dionysus

Wild One, Dancer of the Vine,
Dionysus of the mad-raging night,
Carry me through your ecstasy
To the release of all that binds me
And holds me back.
Show me the joy of your dance,
The marvel of bliss and delight
That is life.
Teach me to empty my cup
Because it is only by emptying
That we can be filled up again.

Fig. 27: Jug with grape design, Akrotiri

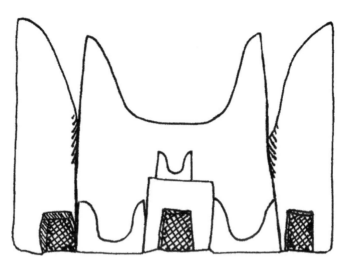

Fig. 28: Sacred horns figurine, Petsofas peak sanctuary

The Horned Ones

Mighty Wild Ones,
Horned Ones of Crete,
Help me to find the strength
In my wildness, my darkness.
Bull and cow,
Billy-goat and nanny-goat,
Stag and doe,
Remind me always
That I am like you:
Animal, yes,
But also much, much more.

The Minotaur

Moon-Bull,
Beloved Minotaur,
As I step through the gateway
Of the sacred horns
To tread the Labyrinth,
Help me to find the center,
The still point
Where all the parts of me
Come together,
Where I remember
That I am no more a monster
Than you are.

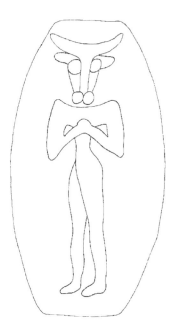

Fig. 29: Agate seal, bull-headed figure, Moni Odigitrias

Fig. 30: Faience plaque, cow suckling calf, Knossos

Europa

Moon-Cow,
Broad face shining,
Who nurtures and nourishes
Your children with
Your divine libations,
Help me to remember
That I, too, can pour out plenty
For myself and others;
The milk of kindness
And generosity
Never sours.

The Minocapros

Wild leaping Horned One,
Sacred Moon-Goat
Who capers from rock to rock
Among hills and mountains,
Lead me down the path
To my own wildness,
The frolicking dance
That breathes beauty
Through my soul
And bids me laugh with the mirth
Of divine joy.

Fig. 31: Detail, Sanctuary rhyton, Zakros

Fig. 32: Faience plaque, goat suckling kids, Knossos

Amalthea

Beloved god-nurse,
Cornucopia-bearer
Whose generosity flows
Through my heart,
Help me to hold this world
With gentle hands
And accept the gifts you give
With an open heart
So that, like you,
I may pour goodness out
Into the world.

The Minelathos

Moon-Stag,
Hunted One
Whose sacrifice feeds
The living and the dead,
Teach me the joy
Of giving myself fully
Heart and soul
So my passion feeds
The very best parts
Of my life.

Fig. 33: Detail, Deer fresco, Hagia Triada

Fig. 34: Late Minoan seal, woman drawing bow

Britomartis

Bright Maiden,
Huntress of the Moon,
Swift of foot and bow,
Help me to find
The strength within me
To chase my deepest desires,
To keep after them
Until I catch them,
Until the hunter and the hunted
Are one.

Serpent Mother

Mystery of Mysteries,
Whose form and shape
We may never know,
Wind your way
Through the tunnels of my life,
That I may understand
The value of the unseen
And the strength
Of the inner shadow
To change the nature
Of the outer world.

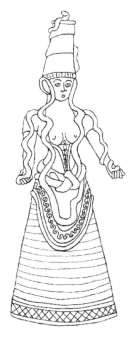

Fig. 35: Faience Snake Goddess figurine, Knossos

Fig. 36: Terracotta bull figurine, Phaistos

Zagreus

I call to the Goodly Bull
Who comes wreathed in blossoms,
Bearing the resurrection of life
For us all.
Oh you who were torn apart
To teach us transformation,
Zagreus,
Show me how to transform myself
From the despair of winter
To the marvel of spring,
From bleak hopelessness
To the power of hope.

The Melissae

I call to the Hive, the Swarm,
The Melissae whose buzzing
Is the sound of the Ancestors' song.
Help me to hear that call
And to honor those
Who have come before me,
On whose shoulders I stand.
Help me to walk their sacred path
And bring honor and compassion
Into the world
In their name.

Fig. 37: Gold bee ornament, Crete

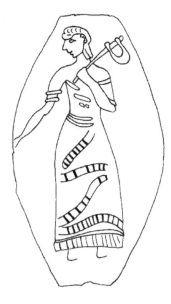

Fig. 38: Hematite seal, robed priest holding mace, Vathia

Minos

Mighty Minos,
King of the Underworld,
Judge of the living and the dead,
Help me to find my own immortality.
Show me the way to move
With the rhythms and the cycles
Of the eternal
So I may understand
My own imperfections
But especially
So I may forgive them in myself
And others.

Eileithyia

Eileithyia, midwife to goddesses and women,
I call to you
Who watches each of us enter this world.
Help me to rebirth myself,
To find again
The innocence and fresh awareness I had
When I began this life.
Teach me your gentle wisdom,
That each day may be a new beginning
And each breath,
A new life.

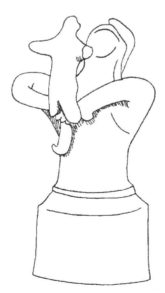

Fig. 39: Bell jar figurine, woman or goddess with infant, Mavrospilio

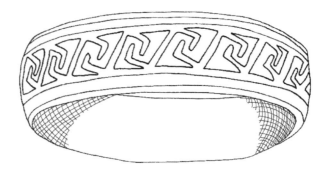

Fig. 40: Gold and lapis ring, Aegina

Daedalus

Cunning Craftsman,
Inventor extraordinaire,
Your name lives on
In the stories mortals tell.
Help me to find my own cunning,
My skill to create
What my life needs
With my hands
And my mind
In service to the divine.

The Daktyls and Hekaterides

Hands of Great Skill,
Crafters all,
You bless the work of the artisan,
Beginner and expert alike.
Help me to fashion beauty
From the raw materials of my life
By the honest work
Of my hands and my mind.
Help me to remember
That the work of my hands
Is as valuable as anything else
I can do.

Fig. 41: Steatite seal, potter making pithos, Sitia

Fig. 42: Detail, stone mold, Sitia

Ourania

Great Cosmic Mother-of-All
I call to you.
My bones are made
Of your stardust;
My soul is born
From your womb.
Help me to remember
That I am a part of you
And you are a part of me,
Both of us
Infinite
Beneath the stars.

Chapter 7:
Create It Yourself

With all the online sources and local metaphysical shops we have access to these days, it's not too hard to find a variety of figurines, candleholders, and other items for your altar. I'll admit that I'm as tempted as the next person by all the 'shinies' out there. But sometimes it's more meaningful to make an item or two by hand for your sacred space. We've found that the Minoan deities are especially pleased by handmade items, either for altar ware or as offerings. Maybe this is because, besides their renown as sailors and traders, the Minoans were also a culture full of artisans.

We may turn to arts-and-crafts when we can't find what we want in a shop, but there are times when putting a little effort into making your own version makes sense even if there are options out there that you could buy. For one thing, it's often cheaper to make your own. And of course, you'll end up with something that's unique, that no one else has. But what's even more important is that as you make your item, you're filling it with your own energy and with the sacred intent you have when you're making it. That's something you just can't buy.

Just like with recipes for food, with craft instructions it's a good idea to read the whole thing through before you start. Gather all your supplies and make sure you have everything on hand before you take the first step. And since these projects can get messy, be sure you have a protected surface to work on (put down newspapers or a dropcloth) so you don't have to scrub paint, glue, or clay off your dining table or desk. Now let's make some Minoan stuff!

Finger Labyrinths

Few of us are lucky enough to have access to a full-size labyrinth that we can walk on a regular basis. Thankfully, there's a smaller version that's more readily available: the finger labyrinth. There are a few brick-and-mortar stores and online shops that carry finger labyrinths made of wood, stone, and ceramic. They range from reasonably priced to very expensive. But you can also make your own. As craft projects go, this one is fairly easy, but it does require some patience. If you can, allow the process of making your finger labyrinth to become a ritual in itself, a sort of moving meditation, so the creation is as special as the finished product.

You can make your finger labyrinth as large or small as you like. Just be sure it's big enough for you to be able to trace the path ('walk' it, so to speak) with your finger without losing your place or getting the lines mixed up. I'm giving you instructions for two different types of finger labyrinths: one that's made of clay and one that's painted on a cloth. The cloth one is especially good for traveling since you can roll it up, tuck it in your suitcase or bag, and not have to worry about it breaking.

I'm not including instructions here, but if you do woodburning and you already have the tools you need, you could burn a finger labyrinth onto a smooth piece of wood (sand well to avoid splinters since you'll be running your finger over it repeatedly). Also, if you're into sewing, it's possible to embroider a finger labyrinth. Simply trace your labyrinth design onto a piece of fabric and embroider along the lines using embroidery floss or yarn that's thick enough to stand out from the surface of the fabric.

Regardless of the materials you use to make your finger labyrinth, you'll need to decide which labyrinth design you want to use. There are dozens out there, from the simple seven-fold labyrinth that's often called the 'Cretan maze' to the fancy Chartres labyrinth design and many others. Take a little time to browse the Internet and your local library until you find the one that's right for you. Just be sure to take into account your own level of patience and attention to detail when you're deciding how complicated your finished labyrinth will be. This project should be enjoyable, not frustrating. And of course, be sure to allow plenty of time. Don't rush the process, but allow it to unfold at its own rate. Creating a labyrinth has an awful lot in common with walking one.

Once you've found the labyrinth design you want to use, you'll want to print out a copy of it on plain paper in the same size that you're planning for your finished finger labyrinth. You'll use this as your template during the creation process.

Clay Finger Labyrinth
Supplies:
Clay: natural air-dry clay, polymer clay, or spice clay (recipe below)
Straight pin, thumbtack, or pushpin
Copy of your labyrinth design on paper
Drying rack for air-dry or spice clay
Baking sheet lined with foil for polymer clay

Using your labyrinth printout as a guide, press or roll the clay to the right size for your finger labyrinth. I like to start with the clay about 1 cm (roughly 1/3 inch) thick. Trim the edges to match your desired shape then lay the paper printout on top of the clay. Be careful to hold the printout steady so it doesn't slide around as you work. You can pin it in place with a couple of straight pins or thumbtacks if you like.

Now take a straight pin, thumbtack, or pushpin and carefully poke through the paper and into the clay along the lines of the labyrinth design. What you're doing here is transferring the design onto the clay as a series of dots. Take your time with this and don't worry if you mess up. You can lift the paper, smooth out the incorrect pinhole, and keep going.

When you've transferred the whole design to the clay, remove the paper and have a look at what you've got. It's a good idea to keep the printout next to the clay as you work so it's easier to visualize the finished design. Now, using the pinholes in the clay as your guidelines, begin to press the clay down along the 'paths' and pinch it up along the 'walls' of the labyrinth to make the grooves and channels. Make sure the path is wide enough to comfortably slide your finger along, since that's how you'll be 'walking' this finger labyrinth. Test it as you go.

Again, take your time with this part of the project. Think about why you're making the labyrinth and what you hope to get out of the experience of using it. Allow your fingers to caress the clay. Enjoy the sensation of touch and the knowledge that you're creating something beautiful and useful. You may want to go back over the design and smooth out any bumps and wrinkles. Try gently 'walking' the whole labyrinth with your finger to be sure you're satisfied with your creation.

Once you're done forming the design, you'll need to finish your finger labyrinth appropriately for the type of clay you're using. For air-dry clay or spice clay, set your labyrinth on a rack (like the kind you would use to cool cookies or a cake) so the air can circulate underneath it and allow it to sit out until it's completely dry. This will take anywhere from several days to two weeks depending on how large and thick your labyrinth is and how high the humidity is. At that point you can paint or varnish it if you like. For polymer clay, set it on a foil-lined baking sheet and bake according to the manufacturer's instructions.

Spice Clay Recipe

1 cup unsweetened applesauce (smooth, not chunky)
¼ cup white glue like Elmer's, not the thick and tacky kind
1½ cups of dried, ground sweet spices (any or all of the following in any proportion as long as you like the scent: cinnamon, cloves, nutmeg, allspice, ginger)

In a large bowl combine the applesauce and glue, stirring until completely mixed. Add the ground spices a little at a time, stirring well with each addition. It will take some elbow grease to get all the spices mixed in since this is a stiff clay. You can mix it with a sturdy spoon or your hands. Once it's all combined, go ahead and make your finger labyrinth right away since this clay will begin to dry out quickly. You can use this spice clay for other projects as well. Just be aware that it works best for thin, flat items; thick objects tend to crack as they dry.

Painted Finger Labyrinth
Supplies:
Fabric or leather
Acrylic paint, paint pens, or permanent markers
Art transfer paper (available at craft and sewing shops)
Copy of your labyrinth design on paper
Ball point pen or sharp pencil

For this type of finger labyrinth, you're going to paint or draw the design on a piece of fabric or leather. I recommend trying your paint or markers on a scrap of your fabric or leather before you start the full project to be sure you'll get the results you want. I've found that most types of fabric work best with regular brush-on paint, but leather will give good results with paint pens and some kinds of permanent markers as well.

If you're not used to working with transfer paper, you might want to test it out on a scrap as well so you know how hard you have to press to transfer your design. You want the transfer to be clear and easy to see, but you don't want to press so hard that you tear the paper or gouge your fabric or leather.

If your fabric has any wrinkles, now's the time to iron it. If you paint over the wrinkles, they'll be almost impossible to remove later on. Ironing might also damage your paint, so be sure to have your fabric nice and smooth before you start painting. If you're using leather and it's wrinkly, your best bet is to press it under a stack of heavy books for a day or two. Don't try to iron it or you might ruin it.

Now lay out your fabric or leather on a firm surface like a table or desk. Lay the transfer or tracing paper on top of it, 'business' side down. Then lay your labyrinth printout (printed side up) on top of the stack. Double-check this—it's very frustrating to draw out a full design, lift up the paper, and discover that you've transferred it to the back of your printout instead of the fabric. It's a good idea to fasten everything together with a few small pieces of tape so nothing slips or slides while you're working.

Next, using the pen or pencil, slowly trace over your labyrinth design, pressing down firmly enough to get a clear transfer. Take your time and take breaks if you need to. As long as you've taped the layers together, you can stop for a bit and come back to it with no problem. When you're finished, carefully remove the tape and lift up the printout and transfer paper. Now it's time to paint!

You can use any color of paint you like, or multiple colors, even metallic ones. If you're feeling especially artistic you can add bits of artwork around the outside of the labyrinth as decorations. If you're painting on fabric, it's a good idea to have a protective layer of cardboard or plastic underneath to keep the paint from staining your tabletop. Leather is usually thick enough that this isn't a problem.

Once you're done, give the paint plenty of time to dry before handling your creation. Now you can finish the edges however you like. Leather can simply be trimmed with sharp scissors. You can finish fabric by sewing a hem, covering the edge with fabric binding, or treating it with Fray-Check sealant so it won't ravel. Now simply enjoy your finger labyrinth!

Labrys and Horns

It's not very hard to find labryses for sale in the form of jewelry and art, but it can be tricky to find one that's big enough to stand up on your altar. And it's virtually impossible to find the labrys-and-horns combination for sale anywhere. So I'm going to give you some basic instructions for creating your own. You can make a plain labrys without a stand, then hang it up on the wall using poster-tack, strong tape, or picture hanging hardware. You could choose to make a labrys with a stand like the ones found in Minoan shrines. Or you could shape the stand like the Minoan sacred horns for your very own labrys-and-horns altar ware.

The project I've described here is a simple arts-and-crafts labrys made from foam core board. You don't need special tools or skills to make it. But if you want to try something a little fancier, most craft shops sell brass and copper metal sheets for jewelry making. You could cut your labrys out of two of these sheets and glue them together over a dowel for a handle. You could even emboss the metal sheets before attaching them together.

As with the finger labyrinth, the first thing you'll need to decide is exactly what kind of design you want to use. Labryses come in a wide variety of shapes, from short and squat to tall and narrow. There are even double labryses with four blades, two on each side. So cruise the Internet and your favorite books until you find a picture you like, then print it out in the size you want your finished labrys to be.

If you're going to make a base for your labrys, find a picture or two of the type of base you'd like to make so you have an image to work from. Then you're ready to begin.

Supplies:
Foam core board (available at craft and office supply shops)
Tape
Ball point pen or sharp pencil
X-acto or craft knife
Dowel for the labrys handle
Card stock or piece cut out of a manila folder (optional, to secure the handle)
Craft glue (the thick, tacky type works best)
Paint (liquid acrylic and spray paint are good choices)
Beads, yarn, or puffy fabric paint (optional, to decorate the labrys)
Air-dry clay (optional, for the labrys stand or horns)
Copy of your labrys design on paper

Begin by making the labrys blade. Lightly tape your labrys printout in place over the foam core board. Trace over the outline of the labrys with the pen or pencil, pressing down hard enough to make an imprint on the foam core board. Remove the printout and cut out the labrys with the craft knife. Take your time with this part. You want the edges to be smooth.

Many Minoan labryses had designs incised into the metal. If you'd like to imitate that, you can either press the design into the foam core board with a ball point pen (the ink will be hidden once you paint the labrys) or apply the design to the surface by gluing on beads or yarn or by outlining the design in puffy fabric paint. Be sure to let your work dry completely before moving on to the handle.

Now attach the handle. If you're using a small dowel that's thinner than the foam core board, you may be able to press it up into the foam. If that's the case, work the handle gently but firmly into the foam core board, no more than halfway through the width of the labrys. If it feels secure, you can just leave it as is. If it feels a little wobbly, gently remove the handle, drizzle a little glue in the hole, and reinsert the handle.

If you're making a large labrys and the dowel is too thick to wedge up inside the foam core board, simply glue it on the back. I don't recommend using tape since it's likely to work loose and become unstable with use. If you want to make it more secure, you can glue a square of card stock over the handle to help keep it tightly in place.

If you're making a plain labrys without a base, you're all done. If you're adding a base, be sure to let the glue dry completely before moving on to the next step.

Use the air-dry clay to make the base. Shape the base separately. Don't put the clay around the labrys handle and try to make it that way. It's much easier to form the base into the shape you want and then insert the handle when you're finished. Again, take your time.

Refer to the pictures you picked out and visualize how big you want the base to be when it's finished. Start with a hunk of clay about the right size and shape it however you like. It doesn't have to be perfect. If you look closely at the ancient Minoan artifacts, you'll see that many of them are uneven and imperfect. Focus on why you're making this item and how you're going to use it when it's finished. Be sure the base is large enough that it will hold your labrys steady and won't tip over. The labrys itself is very lightweight, so this shouldn't be too hard.

When you're satisfied with the shape of the base, leave it standing up on your work surface and gently press the labrys handle into it. I like to press the handle almost all the way to the bottom of the base so it will be steady. Now leave it to dry. How long this takes will depend on how large and thick your base is.

When it's fully dry, inspect your labrys. Chances are, the handle is a little loose because the clay shrank as it dried. Don't panic! Just gently pull the handle out, drizzle in a little glue, and put the handle back in. Let the glue dry thoroughly before moving on.

Now it's time to paint! You can paint the entire assembly a single color or use different colors on the labrys, handle, and base. Metallic paints are especially evocative of the glistening metal labryses from Minoan times. Again, be sure to let your creation dry fully before handling it. Now you have a beautiful addition to your sacred space.

Drop Spindle

Yes, this is a set of instructions to make a drop spindle so you can spin your own yarn. I recommend making two, a top whorl spindle and a bottom whorl spindle, and trying them both to see which you prefer. Both types were common in the ancient world, just as they are today among spinners. Which type any given person likes is usually down to personal preference.

Once you've made your spindle, you'll need fiber to spin. There are a number of online suppliers where you can order wool, cotton, and other fibers all clean and combed and ready to spin. I recommend wool roving as an easy choice to learn with. But if you don't want to go to that expense, you can also save the little wads of cottony material that are stuffed into the tops of pill bottles. This material is usually actually rayon, not cotton, and it spins pretty easily. Check Youtube for "how to spin with a drop spindle" videos—there are plenty of them. Learning to spin is sort of a "rub your stomach and pat your head" kind of activity, but once you get the hang of it, it's quite relaxing and fun. And having your own handspun yarn to use as offerings or in rituals and spellwork is pretty amazing.

Supplies:

Shaft: a wooden chopstick (the kind from takeout food will work just fine) or dowel 8 to 12" (20 to 30 cm) long. If you're using a wooden wheel as the spindle whorl, make sure your dowel is the same diameter as the hole in the middle of the wheel so it fits snugly.

Whorl: this is the weight that helps make the spindle turn easily. A wooden wheel 2 to 4" (5 to 10 cm) in diameter from a craft shop is a good choice. You can also use a block of polymer clay (Fimo, Sculpey, or similar) to make one. If you're using polymer clay, you'll also need an oven in which to bake the whorl.

Small metal screw hook. No bigger than 1/2" (1.25 cm) in diameter.

Awl, pushpin, or power drill. Please don't panic just because I've listed a power tool here. This is to make a pilot hole in the end of the spindle shaft so you can screw the cup hook into it without a fight. If you're using a chopstick, the wood will probably be soft enough that you can just poke a hole in the end of it with an awl or pushpin. A dowel is likely to be made of harder wood that will split if you try to jam an awl or pushpin in it. In this case, a power drill with a very small bit will do the job for you. Either way, you want the pilot hole to be a smidge smaller than the threaded part on your hook.

Begin by making a pilot hole in the shaft. If you're using a chopstick, do this in the wider end (the part you hold rather than the part that touches the food). If you're using a dowel, either end is fine. Now screw in the screw eye until it's secure.

Next up, the whorl. If you're using a wooden wheel, simply slide it onto the shaft. You'll want it 2" (5 cm) from the end with the screw eye for a top whorl spindle or 2" (5 cm) from the other end for a bottom whorl spindle. If my experience making this sort of drop spindle is any indication, it's liable to be a snug fit, so you might have to get forceful to position the wheel where you want it. Twisting the shaft as you go can help. That's it—you're done!

If you're using polymer clay for the wheel, you'll want about 3/4 of a 2 ounce (56 gram) block of clay. Form the clay into a disk that's an even thickness. Flattening it on a hard surface like a counter can help, and you can use a jar lid or other round object to help with the shape. Now find the center of the disk and gently poke the shaft through it to make a hole. You might need to flatten the disk back out again afterward, and that's OK. Don't make the hole too big. You want the whorl to fit tightly on the shaft so it doesn't fall off during use.

Bake the whorl (without the shaft in it) according to the package directions, then let it cool until it's just warm to the touch. If you try to put the spindle together while the whorl is hot, the clay is liable to crack. Wait until it's gently warm, then slide it onto the shaft. As the whorl continues to cool, it will shrink just a little, making the joint more secure. Allow it to cool completely before using. Now go learn to spin!

Chapter 8:
Compendium

The information, rituals, and devotionals in this book are intended as a starting point for your personal spiritual practice. Once you develop a relationship with the Minoan gods and goddesses, you'll want to begin creating your own ways of honoring them.

In addition to what your intuition might tell you, it's helpful to have some practical information to base your ideas on. We actually know quite a lot about ancient Minoan life: what the people wore, what they ate, what kinds of incense and stones they used, and so on. Knowing these things can provide a starting point for setting up your altar or working out the details of a ritual. So I've compiled several lists of items and ingredients we know the Minoans had. You can use this information to help choose altar items, make incense, and cook food for offerings or celebrations. You can also use the list of stones as a starting point for making Minoan-themed jewelry.

Stones the Minoans Used

Agate
Alabaster
Amethyst
Calcite
Carnelian
Chalcedony
Clear quartz (rock crystal)
Garnet
Hematite
Jasper
Lapis
Marble
Obsidian
Serpentine
Slate
Steatite
Yellow jasper

Incense Ingredients
from Minoan Times

Bay leaf
Copal
Cypress wood
Dittany
Fennel seed
Frankincense
Gum mastic
Juniper berries
Labdanum
Myrrh
Oregano
Pine/fir needles
Pine/fir resin
Sage

Food and Drink from Minoan Crete

Beverages
Beer
Cow, goat, and sheep milk
Herbal tea
Mead
Resinated wine (retsina)
Water
Wine

Vegetables
Chickpeas
Fava beans
Leeks
Lentils
Mushrooms
Olives
Onions
Wild artichokes
Wild asparagus
Wild greens (horta)

Fruits
Dates
Figs
Grapes
Pomegranates
Quinces
Raisins

Meats
Beef
Deer
Fish (fresh and salted)
Goat
Grouse
Mutton/lamb
Octopus
Pork
Rabbit
Seafood (limpets, mussels, etc.)
Snails
Squid

Other Foods
Almonds
Barley
Boiled-down grape juice
   (sweetener)
Farmer/cottage cheese
Honey
Olive oil
Pine nuts
Rye
Sea salt
Sesame seeds
Wheat
Whole grain bread
Wine vinegar

Herbs and Spices

Anise
Bay laurel
Coriander
Cumin
Dill
Dittany
Fennel
Garlic
Lavender
Marjoram
Myrtle
Oregano
Parsley
Poppyseed
Rosemary
Rue
Saffron
Sage
Sesame seed
Thyme
Tilia (linden flowers)
Verbena
Wormwood

Chapter 9:
Resources

Of course this book is just the beginning. As you continue your exploration of Modern Minoan Paganism, you'll want more information. You'll want to try new things for yourself. And you'll create your own path, your own unique version of our tradition, as you go.

In this chapter I've included some books and music that you might find helpful for expanding your spiritual practice. There are lots of great resources online and in your local public library as well. You don't have to buy lots of books to learn lots of things! If your library doesn't have a book you're looking for, you can request that they purchase it or get it for you via inter-library loan.

Further Reading

A few of these titles may be out of print, but they're all readily available at used booksellers like ABEbooks and Thriftbooks and are well worth searching out. My books are still in print as of this publication.

Ariadne's Thread: Awakening the Wonders of the Ancient Minoans in Our Modern Lives by Laura Perry. A big section on ancient Minoan religion and culture plus a year's worth of Minoan-style rituals and a lifetime's worth of rites of passage honoring the Minoan deities and the milestones in our lives. Most of the rituals are more suited to groups than solitaries. I wrote this book many years before MMP began, and the rituals reflect the Wiccan environment in which I was working at the time. But the information about the Minoans is valuable, and the rituals can be easily altered to fit within the MMP standard ritual format.

Ecstatic Body Postures: An Alternate Reality Workbook by Belinda Gore. Excellent introduction to the function and practice of ecstatic body postures from cultures around the world and across time, including the Minoans and their ancestors who came from Neolithic Anatolia. Please note that the Realm of the Dead posture as described in this book is incorrect. Though the figurines on which this posture is based are displayed standing upright in museums, they were all found lying down in graves. So lying down with the arms crossed over the abdomen is the correct way to safely use this pose.

Incense: Crafting and Use of Magickal Scents by Carl F. Neal. Good basic instructions for making your own incense—it's not hard at all. Includes descriptions of a wide variety of ingredients and recipes for every imaginable scent and occasion.

Lost Goddesses of Early Greece: A Collection of Pre-Hellenic Myths by Charlene Spretnak. This is an excellent source for what's probably the original version of the Eleusinian Mysteries mythos cycle (the Demeter/Persephone tale) as it was known in ancient Crete.

Minotaur: Sir Arthur Evans and the Archaeology of the Minoan Myth by J.A. Macgillivray. This book is almost painfully honest about Sir Arthur Evans and his narrowminded Victorian mindset, including the racism (extreme even for his time) that caused him so many problems beginning even before he started excavating at Knossos. But it gives an excellent description of Evans' lengthy excavations on Crete and his conclusions, many unsupported, which continue to bias archaeologists and historians to this day. It also provides an enlightening description of the flourishing trade in faux Minoan artifacts that began almost as soon as the excavations began, and provides a reminder that Evans was almost single-handedly responsible for turning the Ashmolean

Museum into the world-class institution it is today. Evans was a complicated man, neither a saint nor a monster, and his work had a profound and lasting impact.

O Mother Sun! A New View of the Cosmic Feminine by Patricia Monaghan. This is a review of Sun goddesses from around the world and the changes that occurred as they were written out of mythology. The information in this book, along with some insightful dance ethnography research, allowed us to find Therasia and incorporate her into our pantheon.

The Ancient and Martial Dances by Arlechina Verdigris. Arlechina is an MMP board member and a professional dance ethnographer who specializes in ancient dances of the Mediterranean. This book traces the roots of ancient Mediterranean Paganism back to the Bronze Age and beyond using the folklore and forms of native dances. A great deal has survived, but in forms that aren't so easy to recognize today. This book teases out those bits and helps us see what's really there. The last chapter, on the symbolism within ancient dance, is especially apropos.

The Chalice and the Blade: Our History, Our Future by Riane Eisler. The author looks to the egalitarian values of ancient Minoan civilization for ways to improve our own modern culture and make it better for everyone. Dr. Eisler looks outside the box of authoritarianism to give us opportunities for building a better future. Her other books are also worth reading in terms of working our way toward more Minoan values of equality and compassion in our modern cultures.

The Double Goddess: Women Sharing Power by Vicki Noble. An exploration of the double goddess motif prevalent in Neolithic and Bronze Age European culture. Twinned and younger/elder goddess pairs show up repeatedly in the Minoan pantheon. Noble's work helped us tease out the younger/elder goddess paradigm and eventually led us to the younger/elder god paradigm as well.

The Goddess in Crete: A guide to 100 Minoan and other sites by Cheryl Straffon and Lana Jarvis, two members of Ariadne's Tribe. A detailed guide to current archaeological sites and museums of Crete, with a focus on the sacred feminine. Includes maps, directions, and other helpful details.

Trance-Portation: Learning to Navigate the Inner World by Diana Paxson. If you're interested in shamanic journeying, this is a great resource for learning the basics on your own both safely and effectively. Though Diana Paxson is known for following a Norse Pagan path, she designed this book so it can be applied to any path or tradition.

Written in Wine: A Devotional Anthology for Dionysos by Bibliotheca Alexandrina. This anthology is based on a Greco-Egyptian view of Dionysus, which comes from many centuries later than Minoan culture. But it's a wonderful exploration of his 'counterculture' aspects that's very appealing for the modern world.

Music

For spiritwork, drumming can help evoke the right feeling and make connecting with the divine easier. Humans have drummed since the Stone Age, so drumming easily calls to mind the sense of ancient times. Here are some of my favorite drumming recordings:

Pretty much everything by David and Steve Gordon, but
     especially *Medicine Drum* and the *Drum Cargo* series
Drumming Inside Mother Earth by Motherdrum
Mother's Heartbeat by Motherdrum
The Spirit of Healing: Shamanic Journey Music by Sandra Ingerman
     and Byron Metcalf

There's a lot of ancient-inspired music out there. You can find chants specifically for MMP on my Youtube channel, including the ones in the standard ritual framework. A lot of us also like to use the music of the groups Daemonia Nymphe (pretty much anything they put out) and Dead Can Dance (specifically the albums *Into the Labyrinth* and *Dionysus*) as background for rituals and meditations.

Index

About the Author

Laura Perry is an artist, writer, and lover of all things ancient and mysterious. The Minoans of Bronze Age Crete have been a particular passion of hers since a fateful art history class introduced her to the frescoes of Knossos in high school. Laura's first book was published in 2001. She continues to write non-fiction and fiction as well as contributing to Pagan anthologies and teaching online courses. She also draws and paints Pagan artwork, including a Minoan-themed Tarot deck. When she's not busy drawing, writing, and editing, she enjoys gardening and giving living history demonstrations at local historic sites.

LauraPerryAuthor.com

Printed in Great Britain
by Amazon

65027252R00156